Anonymous

The fish and game laws of the state of New York,

Also laws for the preservation of the forests, including amendments thereto,

passed in 1888

Anonymous

The fish and game laws of the state of New York,
Also laws for the preservation of the forests, including amendments thereto, passed in 1888

ISBN/EAN: 9783337810917

Printed in Europe, USA, Canada, Australia, Japan

Cover: Foto ©ninafisch / pixelio.de

More available books at **www.hansebooks.com**

THE

FISH AND GAME LAWS

OF THE

STATE OF NEW YORK,

ALSO

Laws for the Preservation of the Forests, Including Amendments thereto, Passed in 1888.

COMPILED UNDER THE DIRECTION OF

THE COMMISSIONERS OF FISHERIES,

BY

GEORGE EDWARD KENT,
Counselor-at-Law, New York City.

THE TROY PRESS COMPANY, PRINTERS.
1888.

COMMISSIONERS OF FISHERIES.

EUGENE G. BLACKFORD,
PRESIDENT AND SHELL-FISH COMMISSIONER,
80 Fulton Market, New York City.

R. U. SHERMAN,
New Hartford, Oneida County, New York.

A. SYLVESTER JOLINE,
Tottenville, New York.

W. H. BOWMAN,
Rochester, New York.

HENRY BURDEN,
Troy, New York.

EDWARD P. DOYLE, CLERK, - Room 311 Potter Building, N. Y. City.
WM. G. FORD, Jr., ENGINEER, - - 80 Fulton Market, N. Y. City.
JOSEPH W. MERSEREAU, STATE OYSTER PROTECTOR,
80 Fulton Market, N. Y. City.

SUPERINTENDENTS OF FISH HATCHERIES.

FRED MATHER, SUPERINTENDENT,
Cold Spring Hatchery, Cold Spring, L. I., N. Y.

SETH GREEN, SUPERINTENDENT,

MONROE A. GREEN, ASST. SUPERINTENDENT,
Caledonia Hatchery, Caledonia, N. Y.

E. F. BOEHM, SUPERINTENDENT,
Sacondaga Hatchery, Mill Creek, Hamilton Co., N. Y.

E. M. MARKS, SUPERINTENDENT,
Fulton Chain Hatchery.

E. L. MARKS, SUPERINTENDENT,
Adirondack Hatchery, Bloomingdale, N. Y.

OFFICERS OF THE FOREST COMMISSION.

COMMISSIONERS.

THEODORE B. BASSELIN, - - - Groghan, Lewis Co.
TOWNSEND COX, - - - - Glen Cove, Long Island.
SHERMAN W. KNEVALS, - - - - New York City.

The Official Post-Office Address of the Commissioners is Albany, N. Y.

SECRETARY.

ABNER L. TRAIN, - - - P. O. Address, Albany, N. Y.

WARDEN.

SAMUEL F. GARMON, - - P. O. Address, Lowville, Lewis Co.

ASSISTANT WARDEN.

WILLIAM F. FOX, - - - P. O. Address, Albany, N. Y.

INSPECTOR.

JOHN B. LOCKE, - - - - P. O. Address, Albany, N. Y.

MESSENGER.

M. J. LONG.

STENOGRAPHER.

Miss JOSEPHINE FOURQUREAU.

FISH AND GAME PROTECTORS.

WILLETT KIDD, - - - - Newburgh, N. Y.
MATTHEW KENNEDY, - - - - Hudson, N. Y.
FRANCISCO WOOD, - - - - Schoharie, N. Y.
SEYMOUR C. ARMSTRONG, - - - Riparius, N. Y.
PETER R. LEONARD, - - - Ogdensburgh, N. Y.
THOS. BRADLEY, - - - - Rockwood, N. Y.
FREDERICK P. DREW, - - - Washington Mills, N. Y.
WM. N. STEELE, - - - - Clayton, N. Y.
JOHN SHERIDAN, - - - - Penn Yan, N. Y.
GEORGE M. SCHWARTZ, - - - Rochester, N. Y.
CHARLES RIPSON, - - - - Youngstown, N. Y.
HENRY C. CARR, - - - - Union Springs, N. Y.
GEORGE MOYER. - - - - Lowville, N. Y.

Two Vacancies.

TABLE OF CONTENTS.

	PAGE.
COMMISSIONERS OF FISHERIES,	3
GAME AND FISH PROTECTORS,	5
THE GENERAL GAME LAW,	10
OTHER GENERAL AND LOCAL ACTS,	31
GAME,	(31 — 39)
FISH,	(39 — 49)
FISH HATCHERIES,	(49 — 51)
SHELL-FISH,	(51 — 76)
FISH-WAYS,	76
FOREST PRESERVE,	82
PENAL CODE,	92
INDEX,	94

THE
FISH AND GAME LAWS

OF THE

STATE OF NEW YORK.

COMMISSIONERS OF FISHERIES.

CHAPTER 285, LAWS 1868, AS AMENDED.

AN ACT to appoint commissioners of fisheries for the State of New York.

SECTION 1. A commission of fisheries for the State of New York is hereby established. Established.

§ 2. It shall be the duty of the commissioners to examine the various rivers, lakes and streams of the State of New York, and the waters adjoining the same, with a view of ascertaining whether they can be rendered more productive of fish, and what measures are desirable to effect this object, either in restoring the production of fish in them, or in protecting or propagating the fish that at present frequent them, or otherwise; and such commissioners shall report the result of their labors, and any recommendations they may have to offer, at the next meeting of the Legislature of this State. (Chap. 285, Laws, 1868.) That it shall be the duty of the commissioners, in addition to the duties imposed upon them by said act, to establish the artificial propagation of shad, white-fish and salmon-trout, in the waters of this State, at such point or points as they may select, and to employ the necessary labor to conduct the same, and to take such other steps toward improving the fisheries of this State as they shall think advisable, at an expense in all, however, not exceeding the sum hereby appropriated. (Added by chap. 567, Laws, 1870.) It shall be the duty of the commissioners of fisheries of the State of New York, to examine the streams of water in the various counties of this State and to take reasonable steps for the propagation of trout, in such streams Duties of commissioners.

as in their judgment can be rendered more productive. (Added by chap. 309, Laws 1879, § 1.)

<small>Commissioners, vacancies, etc.</small>
§ 3. Horatio Seymour, Seth Green and Robert B. Roosevelt are appointed commissioners under this act, to hold office for two years, and a sum of one thousand dollars is appropriated for their necessary expenses in carrying this act into effect, which the treasurer shall pay to them on the warrant of the comptroller, from time to time, as their vouchers for such expenses shall be exhibited and approved. (Sec. 3 of chap. 285, Laws 1868.) All vacancies occurring in said commission shall be filled by the governor of this State, and the term of office is hereby extended three years, the commissioners being required to report yearly on the condition of the fisheries of the State, and the matters under their charge. (Sec. 2 of chap. 567, Laws 1870.) The fishery commission of the State of New York, created by act passed April twenty-second, one thousand eight hundred and sixty-eight (Laws 1868, chap. 285), is continued with the powers conferred upon them by the said act. The commissioners to receive no salary, and to expend only such sums as have heretofore been appropriated or shall hereafter, from time to time, be appropriated for such purpose. (Sec. 1 of chap. 74 of the Laws of 1873.) The governor is authorized to appoint a resident of the counties of either Kings, Queens or Suffolk an additional member of the commissioners of fisheries of the State of New York, and to supply his place, should a vacancy occur therein, as provided in chapter 567 of the Laws of 1870. (Sec. 2 of chap. 309 of the Laws of 1879.)

<small>Shad.</small>
§ 4. No person shall take from the Hudson river any shad at any other time than between the fifteenth day of March and the fifteenth day of June in each year, and every person who shall at any other time, take any shad, or set or draw any net or seine in said river, or aid or assist therein, for the purpose of taking shad, shall forfeit the sum of one hundred dollars to the treasury of the State, and their nets shall be confiscated; provided that nothing in this section shall apply to taking of fish by orders of the commissioners for the purpose of artificial or natural propagation of the same, or when the parties authorized to take fish contrary to the provisions hereof, have stipulated to hatch fish under the direction of the commissioners. (Sec. 3 of chap. 567, Laws 1870.)

<small>Penalties, how recovered.</small>
§ 5. All penalties imposed under the provisions of this act may be recovered with costs of suit, by the commissioners of fisheries in their official name, or by any person or persons in his or their own names, by suit in the supreme court, or any other court

of record in this State. On the non-payment of any judgment, when recovered in pursuance hereof, the defendant shall be committed to the common jail of the county for the period which shall be computed at the rate of one day for each dollar of the amount of the judgment. (Sec. 5, Laws of 1870, chap. 567.)

§ 6. When any pound, weir, or net is liable to be confiscated under any provisions of this act, it shall be the duty of the commissioners either to take possession of the same and employ the necessary agents therefor, subject to an action against them in their official capacity, by any claimant or claimants, on the ground that the same was not liable to confiscation, or they may institute a suit in supreme court or any court of record, for the confiscation of said pound, weir or net, in which case the said court may issue a warrant directing the sheriff to attach and safely hold such pound, weir or net, until said action shall be determined, and the suit shall be tried, and judgment rendered according to the practice usual in cases of an analogous character. (Sec. 6, Laws 1870, chap. 567.) *Pound, weir or nets to be confiscated.*

GAME AND FISH PROTECTORS.

CHAPTER 577 OF THE LAWS OF 1888.

AN ACT to provide for a more effective organization of game and fish protectors.

SECTION 1. There shall be appointed by the board of commissioners of fisheries fifteen game and fish protectors, whose jurisdiction shall embrace the whole territory of the state, and whose powers and duties shall be as hereinafter in this act defined. They shall hold their office respectively during the pleasure of the board of fish commissioners, who may summarily remove any one of their number, whenever in their judgment they shall deem such a change, for any cause, advisable. One of such protectors shall be designated by the said board of commissioners as chief game and fish protector, and the other protectors shall be under his direction and supervision. The chief game and fish protector shall give bond, with sureties, for the sum of one thousand dollars, and each other protector shall give similar bonds for the sum of five hundred dollars, conditioned for the faithful performance of their duties, respectively, such bonds to be subject to the approval of the board of commissioners of fisheries. The chief game and fish protector shall issue to his subordinates such general and special orders *Appointment, powers, salary.*

and instructions in the execution of their duties under the law as he shall deem necessary; and he may in his discretion assign any or all of them to duty in districts to be prescribed by him, subject to the approval of the board of commissioners of fisheries, but such assignment shall not relieve any protector from the performance of duty in any other part of the State where his services may be needed. No protector shall be engaged in any business or employment which will hinder him at any time from attending to his official duties. The compensation of the chief game and fish protector shall be two thousand dollars per year salary, to be paid in monthly installments, and he shall be allowed his actual expenses of travel in the performance of his duty, not exceeding one thousand dollars per year. Each other protector shall receive an annual salary of five hundred dollars, payable in monthly installments, and shall be allowed for his actual expenses of travel in the performance of his duty not exceeding three hundred dollars per year. The chief game protector shall be assigned desk room in the rooms of the commissioners of forestry in the capitol at Albany, which rooms shall be his headquarters, and he shall have authority to employ such clerical service as he shall need at such headquarters, at a cost not exceeding eight hundred dollars per year.

Duties: Power to prosecute. § 2. It shall be the duty of the game and fish protectors to enforce the laws of the State, and the provisions supplementary thereto made by any county board of supervisors, for the protection of game and fish. And for this purpose they shall visit suspected places, and gather such information as may be in their power to do relative to infractions of such laws committed by any person; and they shall have authority to direct the commencement of suits for the violation of any such laws in all cases where they may have cause to believe that sufficient evidence exists to justify such prosecution.

Prosecution, etc. § 3. Such suits shall be commenced on the order of any game and fish protector, in the name of the people, by any district attorney where the offense shall be alleged to have been committed, or by the district attorney of an adjoining county; and such suits shall be prosecuted to determination in the county where they shall be commenced, unless for good cause appearing, a discontinuance shall be directed by the chief game and fish protector; but in no case where such discontinuance shall be directed shall any costs be charged or be chargeable to the prosecution. If it shall appear in any case that the business of the office of the district attorney of any county where suits may be thus commenced is so pressing that the district attorney can not give to such suits prompt and necessary attention, the game and fish protector having authority to direct the prosecution may, with the approval of the chief game and fish protector, employ other counsel in the same county to commence and conduct such suits to termination, with the same authority in the premises that the district attorney would have. The compensation of any such counsel shall be paid on the audit of the chief game and fish protector, out of the penalties and applicable costs recovered in any such case; and where there shall be a failure to recover, or a deficiency of such funds for such payment, then out of any funds that may be applicable to such purpose by the provisions of this act.

§ 4. Witnesses' and other fees and disbursements and full costs shall be included in any judgement in favor of the people, recovered under the provisions of this act, at the rate fixed by section three thousand two hundred and fifty-one of the code of procedure, without reference to the amount of recovery. All money necessary for witnesses' fees and disbursements in any such action, shall, on the requisition of the district attorney, be advanced by, and all moneys, except costs, which shall belong to the district attorney, recovered in any action, and all fines collected, shall be paid to the treasurer of the county in which the actions or proceedings shall have been commenced; and the district attorney or treasurer of said county, upon the payment of any judgment, may satisfy the same of record, as the attorney for the people. One-half of all moneys thus paid into any county treasury, over and above the amount necessary to reimburse the county for any outlays or expenses paid out by the county treasurer under this act, shall be paid, on or before the thirtieth day of September, in each year, into the State treasury, and become and be part of the general fund. And the remaining one-half of all such moneys, over and above the amount necessary to reimburse the county for any outlays or expenses paid out by the county treasurer, under this act, shall be paid to and belong to the game and fish protector who brings, or causes to be brought, the action or proceedings in which such fine or penalty shall be recovered, and shall be paid to him by the county treasurer within thirty days after the same shall be received by him from the district attorney, upon the certificate of the district attorney, or special counsel employed in the case, that such action or proceeding was brought, or caused to be brought, by such game and fish protector. *Fees, costs, disbursements, etc.*

§ 5. The said protectors, or any of them, may, without warrant, arrest any person violating any of the statutes now or hereafter enacted and in force at the time for the protection of moose, wild deer, *Power to arrest.*

birds and fish, or any of them, and take such person before a justice of the peace or police justice, or other magistrate having jurisdiction, who shall proceed without delay to hear, try and determine the matter, and give and enforce judgment according to the allegations and proofs.

Records.
§ 6. Each game and fish protector shall keep a record in which he shall enter daily his official acts and proceedings, and he shall at the close of each calender month make a summary of such record, giving such statements in detail as shall be necessary for the information of his chief, and report such summary and statement to the chief game and fish protector; and no payment of salary or of traveling expenses shall be made by the comptroller to any protector, except upon the certificate of the chief protector, that he has made the report required by this section, and has performed his duty in all respects to the satisfaction of such chief.

Reports: Annual reports, etc.
§ 7. The chief game and fish protector shall promptly report to the board of commissioners of fisheries any cases of neglect or dereliction of duty, or of incompetency, which he shall discover in any of the game and fish protectors, together with any facts he may have to state in connection therewith. He shall also make a report annually to the board of commissioners of fisheries, on the first day of December, of the operations of his department during the preceding year, and shall make such further reports as he shall be called on by such board to make at any time in regard to the business of his department.

Chief protector may apply to attorney-general.
§ 8. The chief game protector shall have authority to apply to the attorney-general for his official opinion upon any question touching the construction and interpretation of the statutes, and the duties of the protectors under the statutes for the protection of game and fish wherein he shall need legal advice, and the attorney-general may, in his discretion, furnish from his office such official legal assistance as he may deem useful in the conduct of any suit brought by any game and fish protector in pursuance of the provisions of this act.

Appropriation.
§ 9. The sum of nineteen thousand dollars, or so much thereof as shall be necessary, is hereby appropriated out of the general fund, to be paid by the treasurer on the warrant of the comptroller, for the purposes of this act for the remainder of the current fiscal year, and the fiscal year to end September thirty, eighteen hundred and eighty-nine.

Acts repealed.
§ 10. Sections, one, three and four of chapter five hundred and ninety-one, laws of eighteen hundred and eighty, and sections one, three and four of chapter three hundred and seventeen, laws of

eighteen hundred and eighty-three, are hereby repealed; but such repeal shall not be held to affect any suit or legal proceedings or right of action existing at the date of the passage of this act.

CHAPTER 317, LAWS 1883.

AN ACT to amend chapter five hundred and ninety-one of the laws of eighteen hundred and eighty, entitled "An act for the appointment of game and fish protectors."

§ 2. Any net, pound or other means or device for taking or capturing fish, or whereby they may be taken or captured, set, put, floated, had, found or maintained in or upon any of the waters of this State, or upon the shores of or islands in any waters of this State, in violation of any existing or hereafter enacted statutes or laws for the protection of fish, is hereby declared to be and is a public nuisance, and may be abated and summarily destroyed by any person, and it shall be the duty of each and every protector aforesaid, and of every game constable, to seize and remove and forthwith destroy the same, and the expense of any seizure, removal and destruction of such net, pound or other means or device as aforesaid, shall be a county charge against the county in which the same shall have been so seized, and shall be paid as other county charges are paid, on the certificate, which shall be final, of such protector, which certificate shall state the time and place of such seizure and destruction, the names of the persons employed therein, the time spent thereabout, and the money advanced, if any, and to whom, and shall be verified by the oath of such protector or person as aforesaid making such seizure and destruction; and no action for damages shall lie or be maintained against any person for or on account of any such seizure or destruction.

Nets, etc., may be destroyed.

THE GENERAL GAME LAW.

(AMENDED TO JULY, 1888.)

CHAPTER 534 OF THE LAWS OF 1879.

AN ACT for the preservation of moose, wild deer, birds, fish and other game.

Wild deer, transporting, trapping, hounding, etc.
SECTION 1. No person shall hunt. kill, chase or take alive any wild deer in any part of the State, save only from the fifteenth day of August to the first day of November in any year, nor shall any one person during such time, kill or take alive more than three deer.

No person, corporation, association, or company shall have in his or its possession in this State, after the same has been killed, any wild deer or venison, save only from the fifteenth day of August to the fifteenth day of November in each year. No person, corporation, association or company shall sell, or expose for sale after the same has been killed any wild deer or venison, save only from the fifteenth day of August to the fifteenth day of November in each year. No person shall, at any time, in this State, kill any fawn, or have in possession the carcass or skin of any such fawn after the same shall have been killed. No person shall, in any part of this State, set any trap, spring gun or other device at any artificial salt lick or other place for the purpose of trapping or killing wild deer. It shall not be lawful to hunt or pursue deer with dogs in any county of this State, except from the first day of September to the twentieth day of October in each year, except in the counties of Queens and Suffolk, when it shall be lawful during the first ten days of October of each year, exclusive of Sunday. It shall not be lawful to pursue deer with dogs in the counties of St. Lawrence and Delaware at any time. It shall be lawful for any person to shoot or kill any dog while in actual pursuit of any deer in violation of the provisions of this act. No person, common carrier, corporation association or company shall at any time carry or transport in this State, or have in possession for the purpose of transportation, any wild deer or venison, taken, caught, killed or captured in the counties of this state, or in either of them, except the counties of Queens and Suffolk, and any person. common carrier, corporation, association or company which has in his or its possession any such wild deer or venison, taken, caught, killed or captured in any of

OF THE STATE OF NEW YORK. 11

the said counties of this State as aforesaid, or in either of them, except the counties of Queens and Suffolk, shall be deemed to have them in possession in violation of this act, except, however, that they may transport or have in possession for the purposes of transportation, from the fifteenth day of August to the fifth day of November, not more than one carcass of wild deer or venison, taken, caught, killed or captured in said counties as aforesaid, or either of them, for each owner of said carcass as aforesaid, provided that such carcass be accompanied by the owner. This section shall not apply to the head or feet of wild deer when severed from the carcass. Any person offending against any of the preceding provisions of this section shall be deemed guilty of a misdemeanor, and in addition thereto shall be liable to a penalty of one hundred dollars for each wild deer or fawn so killed, hunted, pursued or trapped, or for each carcass or part thereof transported or had in possession for transportation in violation of this act, and for every spring gun so set, or wild deer or fawn skin, or venison, had in possession, and may be proceeded against therefor in any county of this State in which the offense was committed, or in which the offender or prosecutor may reside, or have an office for the transaction of business. (As amended by chapter 501, Laws of 1888.)

§ 2. No person shall, at any time or place within this State, take, Moose. chase with dogs, or kill any moose, nor shall any person sell or expose for sale, or have in his or her possession, any moose after the same has been so taken or killed. Any person violating this section shall be deemed guilty of a misdemanor, and in addition thereto shall be liable to a penalty of fifty dollars for each offense.

§ 3. No person shall hunt, kill or take alive any wild deer by the Crusting process or mode commonly known as crusting, or enter any place ing. where wild deer are yarded with intent to kill, take alive or destroy the same at any time. Any person offending against any of the provisions of this section shall be deemed guilty of a misdemeanor, and in addition thereto shall be liable to a penalty of one hundred dollars for each wild deer so hunted, killed, taken alive or destroyed. (As amended by chapter 194, Laws of 1886.)

§ 4. No person shall kill, or expose for sale, or have in his or her Wild duck, possession after the same has been kill, any wild duck, goose, or brant, brant. in any of the waters of this State, between the first day of May and the first day of September, except that in the waters of Long Island none of said birds shall be killed between the first day of May and the first day of October. Any person violating any of the provisions of this section shall be deemed guilty of a misdemeanor, and in addition thereto shall be liable to a penalty of twenty-five dollars for each and every wild duck, goose, or brant killed, or had in his possession; and any person who shall, at any time, kill any of said birds between sunset and daylight, or pursue or fire at any of said birds with the aid of any light or lantern, shall be deemed guilty of a misdemeanor, and in addition thereto shall be liable to a penalty of fifty dollars for each offense against this provision. And any person found between sunset and sunrise on the water with a gun and lantern, in the act of attempting to pursue, fire at, or kill any such birds, shall be deemed guilty of a violation of this section.*

Using swivel or punt gun, net, etc.

§ 5. No person shall, at any time, kill any wild duck, goose, or brant, with any device or instrument known as a swivel or punt-gun, or with any gun other than such guns as are habitually raised at arm's length and fired from the shoulder, or use any net, device or instrument, or gun other than aforesaid, with the intent to capture or kill any such birds. Any person violating any of the provisions of this section shall be deemed guilty of a misdemeanor, and in addition thereto shall be liable to a penalty of fifty dollars.

Floating batteries, decoys, etc.

§ 6. No person shall use any floating battery, machine, or other device, whereby the gunner is concealed, for the purpose of killing any wild fowl, or shoot out of any such floating battery, machine, or device, at any wild goose, brant, or duck, in any of the waters of this State, or use any decoy or construct any bow-house, at a greater distance than twenty rods from the shore, for the purpose of shooting at or killing any such birds. Any person violating any of the provisions of this section shall be deemed guilty of a misdemeanor, and in addition thereto shall be liable to a penalty of fifty dollars for each offense. But nothing in this section shall apply to the waters of the Great South bay, west of Smith's Point, or the waters of Peconic bay, or Shinnecock bay, or Lake Ontario, or the river St. Lawrence, or the Hudson river below Albany.

Using boats, etc.

§ 7. No person shall sail for any wild fowl, or shoot at any wild goose, brant or duck, from any vessel propelled by steam or sails, or from any other structure attached to the same, in any of the waters of this State, except Long Island Sound, Gardiner's and Peconic bays, Lake Ontario and the Hudson river below Iona Island. Any person violating any of the provisions of this section shall be deemed guilty of a misdemeanor, and in addition shall be liable to a penalty of ten dollars. (As amended by chapter 591, Laws 1887.)

---

* See chap. 247, Laws 1886.

§ 8. No person shall kill, expose for sale, or have in posession after the same has been killed, any quail, between the first day of January and the first day of November, except as hereinafter provided; no person shall kill, or expose for sale, or have in posession after the same has been killed, any hare or rabbit, between the first day of February and the first day of November, nor at any time kill or hunt any hare or rabbit with ferrets. This shall not prevent the owners or occupants of nurseries or orchards, in any of the counties of this State, from trapping or hunting hares or rabbits, with ferrets, or otherwise, within the limits of said nurseries or orchards, or any forest or field adjoining such nurseries or orchards, and the posession of any hare or rabbit may be excused by any person proving the same to have been caught or killed within the limits aforesaid. No person shall kill any quail in the counties of Montgomery, Schenectady, Saratoga or Albany, within two years from the passage of this act. Any person violating either of the provisions of this section shall be deemed guilty of a misdemeanor, and in addition thereto shall be liable for any violation of the first provision to a penalty of twenty-five dollars for each quail, hare or rabbit so killed, exposed for sale, or had in possession.* (As amended by chapter 584, Laws 1880.) *Quail, hare. rabbit, ferrets, etc.*

§ 9. No person shall kill or expose for sale, or have in his or her possession after the same has been killed, any woodcock, between the first day of January and the first day of September, in the counties of Oneida and Delaware, and in other parts of the State, between the first day of January and the first day of August in each year, except as hereinafter provided. It shall not be lawful for any person to kill or expose for sale, or to have in his or her possession after the same has been killed, any black or grey squirrel, between the first day of February and the first day of August in each year. Any person violating either of the provisions of this section shall be deemed guilty of a misdemeanor, and in addition thereto shall be liable to a penalty of twenty-five dollars for each bird or animal so killed or had in possession.† (As amended by chapter 269, Laws 1884. *Woodcock,black or gray squirrels.*

§ 10. No person shall kill, or expose for sale, or have in his or her possession, after the same has been killed, any ruffed grouse, commonly called partridge; or pinnated grouse, commonly called prairie chicken, between the first day of January and the first day of Septem- *Partridge, prairie chicken.*

---

*See chapter 542, Laws 1886, in relation to Robin's Island; chapter 395, Laws 1886, in relation to Niagara county.

†See chapter 430, Laws 1886, in relation to Chautauqua and Cattaraugus counties.

14   THE FISH AND GAME LAWS

ber, except as hereinafter provided. Any person violating any of the provisions of this section shall be deemed guilty of a misdemeanor, and in addition thereto shall be liable to a penalty of twenty-five dollars for each bird so killed or had in possession.*

Netting, etc., prohibited.

§ 11. No person shall, at any time or place within this State, take or kill any ruffed grouse, commonly called patridge, or any pinnated grouse, commonly called prairie chicken, or any spruce grouse, commonly called Canada partridge, or any quail, with any net, trap, or snare, or set any such net, trap, or snare for the purpose of taking or killing any of such birds; nor shall any person willfully sell, or expose for sale, or have in his or her possession, any of the said birds after the same shall have been so taken or killed. Any person violating any of the provisions of this section shall be deemed guilty of a misdemeanor, and in addition thereto shall be liable to a penalty of ten dollars for each bird so taken and killed, or had in possession. And it shall be lawful for any person to take and destroy any such nets, traps, or snares, whenever found set.

Eagles, etc.

§ 12. No person shall, at any time, in this State, kill or expose for sale, or have in possession after the same is killed, any eagle, woodpecker, night-hawk, yellow bird, wren, martin, oriole, or any song bird, under a penalty of five dollars for each bird so killed, exposed for sale or had in possession. (As amended by Laws of 1880, chapter 584.†)

Robins, larks and starling.

§ 13. No person shall kill, or expose for sale, or have in possession after the same has been killed, any robin, meadow lark, or starling save only during the months of October, November, December, under a penalty of five dollars for each bird so killed, exposed for sale, or had in possession. (As amended by Laws of 1880, chapter 584.†)

Exceptions.

§ 14. The last two sections shall not apply to any person who shall kill any bird for the purpose of studying its habits or history, or having the same stuffed and set up as a specimen; or to any person who shall kill on his own premises any robins in the act of destroying fruit or grapes.‡

Robbing nests.

§ 15. No person shall willfully destroy or rob the nest of any wild birds whatever, except crows, blackbirds, hawks, and owls, save only where it may be necessary to protect dwelling-houses, or prevent their

---

*See chapter 395, Laws 1886, in relation to Niagara county.

†See chapter 427, Laws 1886, an act for the preservation of song and wild birds, which may operate as a repeal.

‡See chapter 427, Laws of 1886, an act for the preservation of song and wild birds, which may operate as a repeal.

defacement. Any person violating this section shall be deemed guilty of a misdemeanor, and in addition thereto shall be liable to a penalty of five dollars for each offense.*

§ 16. Any person who shall knowingly trespass upon inclosed or cultivated lands, for the purpose of shooting or hunting any game protected by this act, or shall take any fish from private ponds or private streams not stocked in whole or in part by the State, or after public notice has been given by the owner or occupant thereof, or person, association or corporation hiring or leasing the exclusive right to shoot or hunt thereon or fish therein from the owner or occupant, as provided in the following section, shall be liable to such owner or occupant, "or person, association or corporation," in addition to the actual damages sustained, exemplary damages to an amount not exceeding twenty-five nor less than fifteen dollars. (As amended by chapter 243, Laws 1885.) <small>Trespassing.</small>

§ 17. The notice referred to in the preceding section shall be given by erecting and maintaining sign-boards, at least one foot square, upon at least every fifty acres of land upon or near the lot lines thereof, or upon or near the shores or banks of any lake, stream or pond, in at least two conspicuous places on premises, or by the personal service upon any person of a written or printed notice containing a brief description of the premises, the name of the owner or person in possession thereof, and such notice to have appended thereto the name of the owner or occupant, or person, association or corporation having the exclusive right to shoot or hunt thereon or fish therein. Any person who shall tear down or in any way deface or injure any such sign-board, shall be guilty of a misdemeanor, and in addition thereto shall be liable to a penalty of twenty-five dollars. (As amended, chapter 243, Laws 1885.) <small>Notice to be erected.</small>

[§ 3. Nothing in this act contained shall be construed as authorizing the leasing of any of the lands or waters belonging to the State, to any person, association or corporation for a fish or game preserve, except for fish hatching purposes. (Added by chapter 243, Laws 1885, in act amending §§ 16 and 17.)] <small>State lands or waters not to be leased.</small>

§ 18. No person shall at any time kill or catch or attempt to kill or catch any speckled trout, brook trout, salmon-trout or land-locked salmon, with any device save that of angling with line, or rod held in the hand except in Lake Ontario and the Niagara river, and in waters which are wholly private, and in the latter only then by permission <small>Trout, etc.</small>

---

* See chap. 427, Laws 1886, an act for the preservation of song and wild birds, which may operate as a repeal.

of the owner thereof; nor shall any person set or draw any net or seine, or use any set-line or set-pole in any lake, pond or stream inhabited by speckled trout, brook trout or salmon-trout, or land-locked salmon, except in the waters of Lake Ontario; but no net shall be set within one mile of the mouth of the Oswego river, or have, on the shores or waters thereof, except said Lake Ontario, any net, seine, set-line, or other unlawful device for the taking of fish; but this act shall not apply or prohibit the catching of minnows for bait, in the waters of Lake Keuka, adjacent to the shores of Yates and Steuben counties, providing the person using the nets for that purpose shall not set them, and shall only use a net with mesh not exceeding one-half inch; said net not to exceed one hundred feet in length, five feet in depth or breadth at the ends, and ten feet in the center, to be used with ropes not exceeding one hundred feet in length, and shall throw back any trout, bass or suckers, or other game fish taken, and keep only chubs, shiners and alewives, to be used as herein stated. And no person shall at any time, or in any way, catch or attempt to catch any speckled or brook trout, or salmon-trout, or land-locked salmon, through the ice, except in Lake Ontario and the Niagara river, and in waters wholly private. Any person who shall offend against any of the provisions of this section shall be deemed guilty of a misdemeanor, and in addition thereto shall be liable to a penalty of twenty-five dollars for any offenses against any of the provisions of this section, and ten dollars additional for each fish taken. All nets, seines, and other devices forbidden by this section to be used are hereby declared to be nuisances and contraband; and any person finding the same in any place where they are forbidden to be used, is authorized to destroy such contraband articles, and no action for damages shall lie against him for such destruction. The phrase "private waters" is hereby defined for purposes of this and the next section only, to mean ponds or streams fed wholly by artificial sources, or by springs existing upon the same farm or tract belonging to the owner or proprietor thereof; or waters brought by artificial pipes, or channels other than natural, into artificial ponds or reservoirs of the owner or proprietor. (As amended by chapter 618, Laws of 1887.)

Speckled trout, salmon.

§ 19. No person shall catch, or attempt to catch, or kill or expose for sale, or have in possession after the same has been caught or killed, any speckeled trout, brook trout, California trout or brown trout, save only from the first day of April to the first day of September in each year, except in the counties included in the Forest Preserve, established by chapter two hundred and eighty-three of the laws of eighteen hundred and eighty-five, where it shall not be lawful to catch, or attempt to catch or kill, or expose for sale, any speckled trout, brook trout, brown trout and California trout, save only from the first day of May to the fifteenth day of September, and salmon trout and land-locked salmon from the first day of May to the first day of October in each year. Any person who shall at any time catch or take any California trout, speckled trout, brook trout, brown trout, salmon trout or land-locked salmon from any of the waters of this State, less than six inches in length, shall immediately place such trout back in the waters from which it was taken, and shall use due care not to kill or injure the same, and the catching of such fish by intent is hereby prohibited. Nor shall any person sell or expose for sale any of said fish less than six inches in length. No person shall at any time take or catch any speckled trout, brook trout, brown trout, salmon trout, land-locked salmon or California trout, from any of the waters of this State for the purpose of stocking a private or public pond or stream except from the waters of Lake Ontario. No person shall at any time willfully molest or disturb any of the fish mentioned in this section while they are upon their natural spawning beds during their spawning season, except in the waters of Lake Ontario, nor shall any person take any of the said fish, or any spawn or milt from any of said fish while upon their natural spawning beds in any of the waters of this State (except such as are wholly private). Any person violating any of the foregoing provisions of this section shall be deemed guilty of a misdemeanor, and in addition thereto shall be liable to a penalty of twenty-five dollars for each fish so caught, killed, exposed for sale or had in possession during the prohibited season aforesaid ; a penalty of ten dollars for each fish sold or exposed for sale of less than six inches long as aforesaid ; and a penalty of fifty dollars for disturbing or molesting fish upon the spawning beds, or taking spawn or milt therefrom, with twenty-five dollars additional for each fish taken thereon. The foregoing provisions are not to apply to the operations of State or public hatcheries, or to the artificial propagation of said fish by State or public authority; nor to the taking, transportation or possessing of fish-fry thus artificially propagated or disturbed for the stocking of waters. Owners or proprietors of private hatcheries are also exempted therefrom to the extent that they may take fish, spawn or milt in their own private waters, for the purpose of artificial propagation, inclusive of the sale, transportation and possession of fish-fry or spawn thus obtained or propagated for the purposes of stocking waters. In all other respects these provisions are to apply. No officer of the State, nor any person, shall place or deposit in any of the waters of the Adirondack region of this State (so called), any fish, or fish-fry, or spawn, or milt, except speckled trout, brook trout, brown trout, salmon-trout, California trout or land-locked salmon, unless the fish so deposited or placed in such waters are indigenous to the particular water where placed, except that non-preying or non-destructive fish, such as usually constitute food for the species above named, may be therein placed. Any person offending against this provision shall be deemed guilty of a misdemeanor, punishable by imprisonment in a penitentiary or county jail for a period not exceeding eighteen months or shall forfeit a penalty of five hundred dollars, or both, in the discretion of the court, for each fish or spawn deposited in violation thereof. No person, carrier, corporation, association or company shall, at any time, carry or transport or have in his or its possession for the purpose of transportation, any speckled trout, salmon-trout, California trout or land-locked salmon, caught or killed in that portion of this State constituting the Forest Preserve; and any person, carrier, corporation, association or company which has in his or its possession any such trout shall be deemed to have them in possession in violation of this section, provided, however, that they may transport from the Forest Preserve or have in possession for the purpose of transportation, speckled trout, brook trout, brown trout and California trout, from the first day of May to the first day of September, and salmon-trout or land-locked salmon from the first day of May to the first day of October in any year caught or killed in the Forest Preserve, provided that they be accompanied by the owner. Any person offending against this provision shall be deemed guilty of a misdemeanor, and in addition thereto shall be liable to a penalty of fifty dollars for each trout or part thereof had in possession for transportation in violation of this provision, and may be proceeded against in any county of this State in which the offender or prosecutor resides or the offender has an office for the transaction of business. (As amended by chapter 617, Laws 1887.)

§ 20. No person shall kill or expose for sale or have in his or her possession after the same has been caught or killed, any salmon trout, land-locked salmon, or lake trout caught in the inland lakes or waters of this State in the months of October, November, December, January, February and March of each year, and in Lake George the additional month of April. Any person violating any of the provisions of this section shall be deemed guilty of a misdemeanor, and in addition thereto, shall be liable to a penalty of ten dollars for each fish so caught, killed, exposed for sale, or had in possession. (As amended by chapter 617, Laws 1887.)

§ 21. No person shall catch or kill any black bass in the waters of Lake Mahopac, or of Columbia county (or in the waters of Schroon lake or river, or Paradox lake, in the counties of Essex or Warren, or in the waters of Friend's lake in Warren county, or in the waters of Skaneateles lake in the counties of Onondaga and Cayuga, or in the waters of Lake Erie and Niagara river above Niagara Falls, on the American side, between the first day of January and the first day of July) or in Lake George or in Brant lake, in Warren county, between the first day of January and the first day of August, or catch or kill any black bass, Oswego bass, muscalonge or pike perch, commonly called wall-eyed pike, in Oneida lake, between the first day of March and the thirtieth day of May, or in any other waters of the State, between the first day of January and the thirtieth day of May, except in Lake Erie and Niagara river above Niagara Falls, on the American side, where the same shall not be caught, killed or had in possession or exposed for sale in Erie county between the first day of January and the first day of July, but this section shall not apply to salt water bass, unless alive, for artificial propagation, or the stocking of other waters, except that bass and muscalonge may be caught in the St. Lawrence, Clyde, Seneca and Oswego rivers, Lake Ontario and Lake Conesus and in Black lake, in St. Lawrence county, between the twentieth day of May and the first day of January. No person shall catch, kill or expose for sale, or have in his or her possession after the same has been killed, any black bass or fresh-water striped bass, weighing less than one-half pound, or less than eight inches in length from end of snout to end of caudal fin, at any time, nor catch, kill or expose for sale, after the same has been killed, any salt-water striped bass weighing less than one-half pound or less than eight inches in length from end of snout to end of caudal fin, at any time. No person shall expose for sale, or have in his or her possession after the same has been killed, any black bass, Oswego.bass, fresh-water striped bass or muscalonge, save only from the twentieth day of May to the first day of January; except in the county of Erie, where the same may be sold and had in possession only between the first day of July and the first day of January.*
Nor shall any person catch or kill, or attempt to catch or kill, any bull-heads in the waters of Lake George or in the waters of

Black bass musca- longe or pike, catching in certain water, regulated.

Special exemptions.

Bass or musca- longe, sale of.

---

* See chapter 498, Laws 1887.

any of the inlets or creeks emptying into said lake, between the first day of April and the first day of July in any year. Nor shall any person, at any time, catch or kill, or attempt to catch or kill, in the waters of Lake George or in the waters of the inlets or creeks emptying into the same, any fish with any set line, or with any device whatever except that of angling with hook and line held in the hand. Nor shall any person catch or kill any pickerel in the waters of Lake George between the fifteenth day of February and the first day of July in any year. Nor shall any person expose for sale or have in his or her possession any pickerel caught or killed in the waters of said Lake George between the fifteenth day of February and the first day of July in any year. Any person violating any of the provisions of this section shall be deemed guilty of a misdemeanor, and in addition thereto shall be liable to a penalty for ten dollars for each fish. (As amended by chapter 619, Laws 1887).

Lake George; special provision.

Penalty.

Not to apply to several western lakes.

§ 2. This act shall not apply to salmon, trout or land-locked salmon caught in Lakes Michigan, Superior, Huron or St. Clair, or in the waters adjacent thereto or connecting the same. (Added to section 21 by chapter 596, Laws 1887).

Shutting or drawing off water.

§ 22. No person shall catch any bass, trout or other fish, in any of the waters of this State, by shutting or drawing off any portion of said waters, nor shall any person take any fish in the waters of the Tonawanda creek between Moulton's dam, in the county of Genesee, and Cotton's dam, in the county of Wyoming, for a period of five years after the passage of this act. Any person violating this section shall be deemed guilty of a misdemeanor, and in addition thereto shall be liable to a penalty of twenty-five dollars for each offense.

Fishing with nets; bull-heads, eels, suckers, etc.

§ 23. No person shall kill or catch, or attempt to kill or catch, any fish, except minnows, in the waters of Lake Ontario on the American side thereof, for the distance of three miles from the mouth of the Niagara river, or Onondaga, Oneida, Seneca, or Cross lakes, or in any of their outlets or tributaries, or in the American waters of the Niagara river above Niagara Falls, in any way or manner, or by any device whatever, except with that of hook and line, and any person catching or killing any fish, except minnows, in any of the above named waters, shall be liable to a penalty of one hundred dollars for each and every offense. No person shall kill or catch, or attempt to kill or catch any fish, except minnows, bull-heads, eels, suckers and catfish in any of the fresh waters, or in any of the canals of this State or in the American waters of the St. Lawrence river, in any way or manner, or by any device whatever,

OF THE STATE OF NEW YORK.   21

except that of angling with a hook and line, save only in the following waters, namely: The Hudson river below the dam at Troy,* and in Lake Ontario, except Great Sodus bay, Port bay, East bay, in the county of Wayne, Henderson harbor, or Henderson bay, in the county of Jefferson;† and also except in Lake Champlain during the month of October and the first fifteen days of November; and also except in the waters of the Walkill river within the county of Ulster, wherein it shall be lawful for any person or persons of one and the same family or household to possess and fish for suckers and eels in the waters of said river during the months of March and April and October and November, with a single fyke, the meshes of which shall not be less than one inch. And also except all that part of the waters of Lake Ontario, together with its bays and inlets, lying and being in the county of Jefferson, and in that part of Oswego county lying between its Jefferson county line and the westerly line of the town of Mexico, and within one-half mile of the outlet or mouth of Salmon river, saving and excepting the shoals adjacent to Henderson bay, on the lake side from the main shore to and including Smoke island, except during the months of November and December, which waters are hereby released from the operation of the provisions of sections twenty-three and twenty-six of the act hereby amended; provided, further, that in Black lake, Mud lake and Yellow lake, in St. Lawrence county, bull-heads, eels, suckers, catfish and pickerel may be killed with a spear, except in the months of March, April and May. No person shall knowingly sell or purchase, or have in his or her possession, any fish killed, caught or taken from any such waters, contrary to the provisions of this section. And any person violating the provisions of this section shall be deemed guilty of a misdemeanor, and in addition thereto shall be liable to a penalty of twenty-five dollars for each and every such offense. And all nets, seines, traps, weir and other devices forbidden by this section are hereby declared contraband, and any person finding the same in any place where they are forbidden is hereby authorized to destroy such contraband article, and no action for damages shall lie against him for such destruction. (As amended by chapter 127, Laws 1884.) _{Nets, etc., contraband.}

§ 24. Any person having in his or her possession upon any of the waters of this State, or upon the shores of or islands in any waters of this State, inhabited by salmon trout, lake trout, black bass, Oswego _{Possession of nets on shore.}

---

*See chapter 247, Laws 1884, railway trestles, etc.; see chapter 522, Laws 1886, pound and purse nets; see chapter 567, Laws 1870, as to shad.

†See chapter 141, Laws 1886, and chapter 366, Laws 1867.

bass, fresh-water striped bass or muscalonge, without the permission of the Commissioners of Fisheries, any snares, nets, stake poles or other device used in unlawfully taking such fish, shall be deemed guilty of a misdemeanor, and in addition thereto shall be liable to a penalty of twenty-five dollars; but nothing herein contained shall apply to that portion of the Hudson river south of the dam at Troy, or to Lake Ontario, or to the waters of the Walkill river in Ulster county. (As amended by chapter 11, Laws 1886).

Polluting streams. § 25. No person, association, company or corporation shall throw or deposit, or permit to be thrown or deposited, any dye stuff, coal tar, refuse from gas houses, saw dust, lime or other deleterious substance, or cause the same to run or flow into or upon any of the rivers, lakes, ponds, streams, or any of the bays or inlets adjoining the Atlantic ocean within the limits of this State. Any person who shall violate this section, or any member of any such company, association or corporation who shall authorize and direct any such violation, shall be guilty of a misdemeanor, and in addition thereto shall be liable to a penalty of fifty dollars for each offense. But this section shall not apply to streams of flowing or tide water, nor to the town of French Creek, in Chautauqua county, which constitutes the motive power of the machinery or manufacturing establishments, when it is absolutely necessary for the manufacturing purposes carried on in such establishments to run the refuse matter and material thereof into such stream. (As amended by chapter 430, Laws 1881. See also chapter 300, Laws 1886, *post.* See Cartwright v. Canandaigua Gas Light Co., 32 Hun, 403, Supreme Court, 4th Dept., March, 1884.)

Meshes, fykes, pounds, nets, etc. § 26. No person shall fish in any of the waters or canals of this State with seines, gill-nets or fykes, the meshes of which shall be less than two and one-half inches, except in the waters excepted in the first section of this act and except in the following waters: In the waters over which Richmond county has civil jurisdiction, the meshes shall not be less than two inches; in the bays and salt waters, estuaries and rivers of Long Island, not less than two and one-half inches, but this prohibition shall not apply to nets used in taking "menhaden" nor to ponds where they are permitted by law; in Lake Erie and Lake Ontario, the meshes shall not be less than four and one-half inches; in the Hudson river between long dock at Piermont in the county of Rockland and the dam at Troy, the meshes shall not be less than two inches except seines, fykes or other nets used in catching bait fish; in Coney Island creek to the mouth thereof extending out into Gravesend bay one-half mile each way, the meshes of which shall be four inches square, except that for eel and flounder fishing, hoop nets, with suitable meshes, may be used within said bay between the fifteenth day of October and the first day of April. No person shall set or take any fish by any device known as pound or trap-net in the waters of Great South bay, except so much thereof as is within the jurisdiction of the town of Islip and not included in the Brookhaven and Smith patents, and the waters of Lake Erie, or bring any fish so taken in such waters to the shore, along the same, or be engaged in procuring or preparing for market any such fish or any part thereof, or exposing fish taken in such nets for sale, in the counties bordering on such waters. Nothing in this section shall be construed as permitting the drawing of seines in the waters of the Hudson between the upper dock at the village of Sing Sing and Croton Landing, in the town of Cortland, nor in any of the waters between the above named points, nor in any portion of the Croton river, between the first day of June and the first day of October of any year, which drawing is hereby expressly forbidden, except that set nets and seines of meshes of one-half inch, may be used in any part of the Croton river and the bay in the Hudson river, lying between Croton point and the village of Sing Sing, from October first to May first of any year, for the purpose of catching smelts and frost fish, but for no other purpose. Nor shall anything in this section be construed to prevent setting of fykes in the Walkill river in Ulster county, during the months of March and April and October and November. Any person violating the provisions of this section shall be deemed guilty of a misdemeanor, and in addition thereto shall be liable to a penalty of fifty dollars. (As amended by chapter 237 of the Laws of 1885.) *Penalty.*

§ 27. Any owner or owners or lessee or lessees of lands or lands and water, whether such owner or owners, lessee or lessees be an individual or individuals, association or associations, society or societies, corporation or corporations, or any person, association or corporation having the exclusive right to shoot or hunt thereon or fish therein, desiring to lay out, devote or dedicate such lands or lands and water for the purpose of a private park or territory for propagating or protecting fish birds or game, shall publish at least once a week for three months, in a paper of general circulation printed in the county or counties within which such lands or lands and water are situated, a notice substantially describing the same, or containing a diagram showing substantially the location of said lands or lands and water. And there shall be inserted in said notice, so published, a clause *Land owners, etc., to publish notice.*

declaring that such lands or lands and water will be used as a private park for the purpose of propagating and protecting fish, birds and game; and it shall be the duty of such owner or owners, lessee or lessees, or person, association or corporation having such exclusive right to shoot or fish at any time during the publication of said notice, or within six months after the final publication thereof, to post or put up notices or sign boards warning all persons against trespassing upon such private territory, which notices or sign boards shall not be less than one foot square, and placed not more than forty rods apart along the entire boundary of said private park or territory, when the same shall consist entirely of land, and when said private park or territory shall consist of both land and water, the notices aforesaid shall be placed in conspicuous places upon said territory so there shall be at least one notice or sign board so placed or erected for every one hundred acres of said territory. And when the property to be protected shall consist of a lake or pond only, said notices shall be placed in at least four conspicuous places upon the shore of such lake or pond. But when said territory, or any part thereof, shall be inclosed by a fence or fences of reasonable capacity, for protection of said premises, then notices or sign boards of the dimensions aforesaid shall be placed on said fence or fences not more than one-half mile apart. After any such territory shall be dedicated and designated as aforesaid, all fish, birds and game of, in or upon said territory, shall be the property of the owner or owners, lessee or lessees thereof, or of the person, association or corporation having the exclusive right to shoot, hunt or fish thereon. (As amended by chapter 623, Laws of 1887.)

Rights of owners of designated parks.

§ 28. After any such territory shall have been dedicated and designated as a private park in such manner as to render such fish or game private property, no person shall catch or take from or kill any fish, birds or game in or upon said grounds or the waters thereon, or put on such grounds or in any such waters, any poisonous or other deleterious substance, or pisciverous fish, or let off the waters from said grounds, with intent to take fish, or to destroy the fish or eggs placed in such waters, or deface or destroy any sign or notice posted or put up as aforesaid, or place any object against or near such fence or enclosure, with the intent to aid dogs or other animals to get into said grounds or to enable animals kept therein to escape therefrom, or enter upon any such ground with the implements or weapons for catching, taking or killing fish, birds or game with the intention of catching, taking or killing any fish, birds or game

Gaming or fishing in private parks.

OF THE STATE OF NEW YORK.

thereon, except that the person, association or corporation having the exclusive right to shoot, hunt or fish thereon, or any person possessing a written permit from such person, association or corporation, shall have the right to shoot or hunt on said lands and fish in said waters, and to enter upon said lands with dogs and kill and take birds or game and catch and take fish therefrom. Any person found guilty of any offense against this section shall be deemed guilty of a misdemeanor, and in addition thereto, shall be liable to the owner or lessee or to the person, association or corporation having the exclusive right to shoot, hunt or fish thereon, in addition to the actual damages incurred, in exemplary damages to the amount of twenty-five dollars. (As amended by chapter 623, Laws of 1887.)

§ 29. The commissioner of fisheries of this State are hereby required and directed to erect and maintain, at a distance of eighty rods from any fishway established or constructed by the State, in any stream or water-course within its boundaries, sign-boards, on which shall be plainly painted or inscribed the words following, to wit: "Eighty rods to the fishway; all persons are by law prohibited from fishing in this stream between this point and the fishway;" said sign-board to be erected on both sides of the stream, above and below the fishway. *Sign-board near State fishways.*

§ 30. No person shall catch, take or kill, or attempt to catch, take or kill, with any implements or device whatever, any fish within a distance of eighty rods from any fishery established by the State, within any stream or water-course within its boundaries, or tear down or deface or destroy any sign-board but up by the commissioners of fisheries of this State. Any person violating any of the provisions of this section, providing the sign-boards mentioned in the preceding section shall have been erected and maintained as directed by this act, shall be deemed guilty of a misdemeanor, and in addition thereto shall be liable to a penalty of twenty-five dollars. *State fisheries. Fishing within eighty rods prohibited.*

§ 31. A State bounty of thirty dollars for a grown wolf, fifteen dollars for a pup wolf, and twenty dollars for a panther, shall be paid to any person or persons who shall kill any of said animals within the boundaries of this State. The person or persons obtaining said bounty shall prove the death of the animal so killed by him or them, by producing satisfactory affidavits, and the skull and skin of said animal, before the supervisor and one of the justices of the peace of the town within the boundaries of which the said animal was killed. Whereupon said supervisor and justice of the peace, in the presence of each other, shall burn and destroy the said skull, and brand the *Bounty for wolves and panthers. Proof to be presented.*

Bounty, how paid.
said skin so that it may be thereafter identified, and issue to the person or persons claiming and entitled to the same, an order on the treasurer of the county to which said town belongs, stating the kind of animal killed, the date of killing of the same, and the amount of the bounty to be paid in virtue of the within section of this act, and the county treasurers of this State are hereby authorized and directed to pay all orders issued as aforesaid; and all orders issued in the manner aforesaid, and paid by the treasurer of any county in this State, shall be a charge of said county against the State, the amount of which charge, on delivery of proper vouchers, the comptroller is hereby authorized and directed to allow in the settlement of taxes due from said county to the State.

Hunting on Sundays prohibited.
§ 32. There shall be no shooting, hunting, trapping or caging of birds or wild beasts, or having in possession in the open air for such purpose the implements for the shooting, hunting, trapping or caging of the same, on the first day of the week, called Sunday; and any person violating either of the provisions of this section shall be deemed guilty of a misdemeanor, and in addition thereto shall be liable to a penalty of twenty-five dollars for every such offense. (See sections 265, 269, Penal Code).

Penalties, how recovered.
§ 33. All penalties imposed by this act may be recovered, with costs of suit, by any person in his own name, or by any society in its name, upon such society giving security for costs, before any justice of the peace in the county where the offense was committed, or in an adjoining county, when the amount does not exceed the jurisdiction of such justice, or when such suit shall be brought in the city of New York, before any justice of the district court, or of the marine court of said city; and such penalties may be recovered in the like manner in any court of record in the State; but on recovery by the plaintiff in such case for a less sum than fifty dollars, the plaintiff shall only be entitled to costs to an amount equal to the amount of such recovery; and it shall be the duty of any district attorney in this State, and he is hereby required to prosecute, or to commence actions, in the name of the people of this State, for the recovery of the penalties allowed hereby, upon receiving proper information; and in all actions brought by such district attorney, one-half of the penalty recovered shall belong to persons giving information on which the action is brought, and the other half shall be paid to the treasurer of

Judgments, how enforced.
the county in which such action is brought. All judgments recovered in pursuance of the provisions of this act, with the interest thereon, may be collected, and the payment thereof enforced by execution

against the person; and any person imprisoned upon any such execution shall be so imprisoned for a period of not less than five days, and at the rate of one day for every dollar or fractional part thereof of such judgment and interest when the same exceeds five dollars; and such imprisonment shall not be satisfaction of such judgment; but no person shall be more than once imprisoned upon any such judgment or execution, and two or more penalties may be included in the same action.

§ 34. Any person who shall be found guilty of a misdemeanor under any of the provisions of this act shall, upon conviction, be punished by a fine of not less than five dollars, nor more than at the rate of one dollar for every dollar of the penalty provided by the section so violated, when the same exceeds five dollars, or by imprisonment in the county jail or penitentiary for a period of not less than five days, nor more than at the rate of one day for every dollar of any such penalty, or by such fine and imprisonment, in the discretion of the court. *Misdemeanors, how punished.*

§ 35. Courts of special sessions in towns and villages, and the several courts in cities having jurisdiction to try other misdemeanors, shall have jurisdiction to try offenders in all cases occurring under this act in the same manner as in other cases where they now have jurisdiction, and to render and enforce judgment accordingly. All fines recovered by the provisions of this act shall be paid over by the court receiving the same to the treasurer of the county wherein the offense was committed, except in the county of New York, and in the county of New York to the chamberlain in the city of New York, within ten days after their reception by such court, and such moneys shall be kept by such treasurer or chamberlain as a separate fund, to be applied to the enforcement of the provisions of this act, in such manner as the board of supervisors of the several counties, except in the city and county of New York, and in such city and county the board of aldermen may direct, either for the employment of special detectives or the payment of rewards for the detection and arrest of offenders, and each of the boards of supervisors of this State shall have power to raise by tax, in the same manner as other taxes are raised for county purposes, such sum, not exceeding one thousand dollars in any year, as they shall deem proper to further aid in the enforcement of the provisions of this act. It shall be the duty of every sheriff, under-sheriff, deputy sheriff, officer of police or policeman, and of every constable and every game constable, and every bay constable to arrest, wherever found within this State, without warrant, any person whom they shall find *Courts, fines, jurisdiction. Supervisors may raise tax to enforce law. Duty of sheriffs, etc.*

violating any of the provisions of this act. and immediately to bring such offender before the nearest magistrate having jurisdiction of the offense for examination and for trial. Any officer or magistrate who shall neglect or refuse diligently to enforce the provisions of this act, upon proper information and complaint, shall be deemed guilty of a misdemeanor, and shall be punished by a fine or imprisonment, or by both such fine and imprisonment in the discretion of the court.

Penalty for failure to enforce law.

§ 36. Any person may sell or have in possession any hare or rabbit or any woodcock, any ruffed grouse commonly called partridge, any pinnated grouse commonly called prairie chicken, and any black or gray squirrel during the month December, and any quail from the first day of January to the first day of February, and any fresh venison from the fifteenth day of November to the fifteenth day of December, and shall not be liable for any penalty under this act, provided he proves that such game was lawfully killed during the periods allowed by this act and not transported contrary to the provisions thereof. (As amended by chapter 194, Laws 1886.)

Rabbit, partridges woodcock, squirrels, etc., possession of, during certain periods authorized.

§ 37. It shall be lawful for the board of supervisors of any county, at their annual meeting, to make any regulations or ordinances protecting other birds, fish or game than those mentioned in this act, and also for the further protection of such birds, fish or game as are in this act mentioned, except wild deer, and to this end to prohibit hunting or fishing in particular localities or waters lying within their respective counties, for limited periods and during certain months of the year, and to prescribe punishments and penalties for the violation thereof, and adopt all necessary measures for the enforcement of such punishment and the collection of such penalties. And such regulations and ordinances shall be published in the papers in such county in which the session laws are published; and a certified copy thereof shall be filed in the office of the clerk of the county; provided, however, that nothing herein contained shall be construed as conferring upon the board of supervisors of any county the right or authority to prohibit the owner or owners, in whole or in part, of lands and waters wholly private, or the lessee or lessees thereof, whether such owner or owners, lessee or lessees be an individual or individuals, association or associations, society or societies, corporation or corporations, from angling and taking fish in a lawful manner during the months now allowed by the laws of this State. This act is intended to apply only to such owner or owners, in whole or in part, of lands and waters, or the lessee or lessees thereof,

Supervisors may make ordinances for protection of fish, game, etc.

Publication of, etc

Proviso.

To whom to apply.

OF THE STATE OF NEW YORK.   29

who shall have complied with the provisions of section twenty-seven of said chapter five hundred and thirty-four of the Laws of eighteen hundred and seventy-nine, and the acts amendatory thereof. (As amended by chapter 212, of the Laws of 1884).

§ 38. It shall be lawful for the boards of supervisors of the several counties of this State, except as by this section hereinafter further provided as to the county of Kings, by the affirmative vote of a majority of the members elected, at a regular meeting of such boards, respectively, to authorize the election in each or any of the towns or cities of their respective counties of one or more officers to be designated game constable, who shall be chosen at town meetings as other town officers are chosen, and hold office for the term of one year; and he or they shall take the oath of office the same, and be invested with and have the same powers in serving process under this act, that town constables now possess in serving civil process; but such game constable for the entire county of Kings may be appointed by the board of supervisors at any regular meeting, and he or they shall hold office to the last day of December next after his appointment, and until his successor shall be appointed and qualified; and all suits prosecuted by such game constable for the county of Kings, for penalties under the provisions of this act, may be prosecuted in the county court of Kings county, or in the city court of Brooklyn; and in case a recovery shall be had in such suits for less than fifty dollars, the plaintiff shall be entitled to costs to the amount of such recovery. Warrants of arrest may be issued by such courts in such actions prosecuted by the game constable of Kings county, as in cases provided for by section one hundred and seventy-nine of the Code of Procedure, except that no undertaking shall be required on behalf of the plaintiff, and the judgments may be enforced by execution against the person, and the sheriff of said county shall not be entitled to any deposit or pay from the plaintiff under the provisions of chapter eight hundred and thirteen of the laws of eighteen hundred and sixty-nine. It shall be the duty of the game constable, after reliable information, to prosecute all violations of this act, and he shall receive such compensation for his services as is allowed by law for like services to constables of towns, and also one-half of all penalties recovered by him for violations of this act. In cases of neglect or refusal of any game constable to prosecute any such violation, he shall forfeit the penalty of twenty-five dollars, to be sued for and recovered as specified in this act. Whenever any game

Costs when game constable fails.

constable shall fail to recover the penalty in any prosecution commenced by him pursuant to this section, the cost of suit incurred by him shall be charged against the county, and it shall be the duty of the board of supervisors of the county to audit and allow the same, as other county charges are audited and allowed. (As amended by chapter 595, Laws 1872.)

Issue of warrants of arrest.

§ 39. Any justice of the marine or district court in the city of New York, or any justice of the peace, police or other magistrate, upon receiving sufficient security for costs on the part of the complainant, and sufficient proof by affidavit that any of the provisions of this act have been violated by any person being temporarily within its jurisdiction, but not residing there permanently, or by any person whose name and residence are unknown, is hereby authorized to issue his warrant for the arrest of such offender, and to cause him to be committed or held to bail to answer the charge against him; and any such justice or magistrate, upon receiving proof or probable cause for believing in the concealment of any game or fish mentioned in this act, and taken during any of the periods prohibited, and upon the complainant's giving security, to be approved by such magistrate, for the damage which the defendant in the case may sustain in consequence of the complaint, provided he shall be found not to have violated the law, shall issue his search warrant and cause search to be made in any house, market, boat, car or other building, and for that end may cause any apartment, chest, box, locker, crate or basket to be broken open and the contents examined.

Search warrant.

Repeal.

§ 40. All acts and parts of acts for the preservation of wild deer, birds, fish and game, including section 2 of chapter 183 of the Laws of 1875, are hereby repealed, except such acts and parts of acts as relate to the commissioners of fisheries, and the establishment of fishways, the construction of dams across the rivers of this State, the protection and preservation of shell-fish, the incorporation of any company for the protection and propagation of fish and game, the election of bay constables, the laws conferring upon the boards of supervisors special powers to legislate for the protection of fish, birds and game, and the laws regulating shad fishing; saving, nevertheless, so much of said acts as may be necessary to sustain any right of recovery or condition thereunder for actions or prosecutions heretofore commenced.

Penalties, to whom paid.

§ 41. One moiety of the penalties herein before prescribed, shall be given to the informant, upon conviction of the offender or offenders, and the collection thereof. It shall be lawful to fish through the ice and to take fish, except trout, black bass and pike, with spear and set lines, in the waters of Seneca lake, Lake Keuka and Canandaigua lake (As amended by chapter 618, of the Laws of 1887; N. Y. Assoc., etc., *v.* Durham, Super. Ct. [J. & S.], 306.

Fishing through the ice and spearing fish in certain lakes.

CHAPTER 531, LAWS OF 1880.

§ 6. Any action brought or prosecuted by any district attorney, pursuant to the provisions of the act hereby amended, may be discontinued by such district attorney, and neither costs nor disbursements in such action shall be recovered by any defendant therein. *Actions by district attorneys.*

§ 7. No person shall take, catch or kill any California trout in any of the waters of this State, in any way or by any device, between the fifteenth day of May and the first day of September. No person shall knowingly sell or purchase or have in possession any California trout killed, taken or caught in the waters of this State during the period aforesaid. Any person violating the provisions of this section shall be deemed guilty of a misdemeanor, and in addition thereto shall be liable to a penalty of twenty-five dollars for each offense. *Not to catch California trout. Penalty.*

§ 2. Game constables, constables, sheriffs and deputy sheriffs, shall have the same powers as are conferred upon game protectors for the enforcement of the provisions of chapter five hundred and thirty-four of the Laws of eighteen hundred and seventy-nine and the amendments thereto, and shall be entitled to the same fees therefor. (Sec. 2 of chap. 429, Laws 1886.) *Constables, sheriffs, etc., powers under game laws.*

OTHER GENERAL AND LOCAL ACTS,

AS AMENDED TO DATE.

GAME.

CHAPTER 361 OF THE LAWS OF 1879.

AN ACT for the preservation of song and small birds.

SECTION 1. No person shall kill, wound, trap, net, snare, catch with bird lime, or with any similar substance or drug, or in any other manner capture, or sell, or expose for sale or transport, during the months of April, May, June, July, August, September or October in any year, any bird of song, or any linnet, blue bird, yellow hammer, *Song birds and certain others, when not to be killed, etc.*

yellow bird, thrush or woodpecker, cat bird, pewee, swallow, martin, blue jay, oriole, kildee, snow bird, grass bird, gross beak, phœbe bird, humming bird, black bird, wren, excepting birds bred in a cage or imported from Europe or the southern United States. No person shall kill or expose for sale, or have in his possession after the same has been killed, any robin, meadow lark, or starling between the first day of January and the fifteenth day of October, save only when such birds are killed on premises of the person killing, and while they are destroying fruit. This section shall not apply to any person who shall kill any bird for the purpose of studying its habits or history or having the same stuffed and set up as a specimen. This act shall apply only to the counties of New York, Kings, Albany, Richmond and Rensselaer.

Robins, meadow larks and starling.

Exceptions.

Application of act.

Penalty. § 2. Any person violating this act shall be deemed guilty of a misdemeanor, punishable by imprisonment in the county jail or penitentiary, of not less than five or more than thirty days, and shall also be liable to a penalty of fifty dollars, to be recovered with costs, by any person suing therefor in his own name.

Penalties, how distributed. § 3. In all actions for the recovery of penalties under this act, one-half of the recovery shall belong to the plaintiff, and the remainder shall be paid to the county treasurer of the county where the offense is committed, except if the offense be committed in the city and county of New York then said remaining half penalty shall be paid to the chamberlain of said city.

(Sections 1, 2 and 3 included in N. Y. City Consolidated Act, L. 1880, Ch. 410; see Commissioners' Reports of 1881 and 1882, p. XVII.)

CHAPTER 427, LAWS 1886.

AN ACT for the preservation of song and wild birds.

Killing, catching or sale of certain song and wild birds prohibited. SECTION 1. No person in any of the counties of this State, shall kill, wound, trap, net, snare, catch with bird lime, or with any similar substance, poison or drug, any bird of song or any linnet, blue bird, yellow hammer, yellow bird, thrush, woodpecker, cat bird, pewee, swallow, martin, blue jay, oriole, kildee, snow bird, grass bird, gross beak, bobolink, phœbe bird, humming bird, wren, robin, meadow lark, or starling, or any wild bird, other than a game bird. Nor shall any person purchase, or have in possession or expose for sale any such song or wild bird, or any part thereof, after the same has been killed. For the purposes of this act the following only shall be considered game birds: The Anatidæ, commonly known as swans, geese, brant, and river and sea ducks; the Rallidæ, commonly known as rails, coots, mud-hens and galli mules; the Limicolæ, commonly known as shore birds, plovers, surf-birds, snipe, woodcock, sand pipers, tatlers and curlews; the Gallinae commonly known as wild turkeys, grouse, prairie chickens, pheasants, partridges and quails. *"Game birds" defined.*

§ 2. No person shall take or needlessly destroy the nest or eggs of any song or wild bird. *Nests or eggs.*

§ 3. Sections one and two of this act shall not apply to any person holding a certificate giving the right to take birds, and their nests and eggs for scientific purposes, as provided for in section four of this act. *Scientific use, exemptions for.*

§ 4. Certificates may be granted by any incorporated society of natural history in the State through such persons or officers as said society may designate, to any properly accredited person of the age of eighteen years or upward, permitting the holder thereof to collect birds, their nests or eggs, for strictly scientific purposes only. In order to obtain such certificate, the applicant for the same must present to the person or persons having the power to grant said certificates, written testimonials from two well-known scientific men, certifying to the good character and fitness of said applicant to be entrusted with such privilege ; must pay to said persons or officers one dollar to defray the necessary expenses attending the granting of such certificates ; and must file with said persons or officers a properly executed bond, in the sum of two hundred dollars, signed by two responsible citizens of the State as sureties. This bond shall be forfeited to the State, and the certificate become void upon proof that the holder of such a certificate has killed any bird, or taken the nest or eggs of any bird for other than the purposes named in sections three and four of this act, and shall be further subject for each such offense to the penalties provided therefor in sections seven and eight of this act. (As amended by chapter 373, Laws 1887.) *Certificate to collect birds, eggs, etc., for science, how granted. Conditions thereof. Penalties for violation of act.*

§ 5. The certificates authorized by this act shall be in force for one year only from the date of their issue, and shall not be transferable. *Term thereof.*

§ 6. The English or European house sparrow (Passer domesticus), is not included among the birds protected by this act, and it shall be considered a misdemeanor to intentionally give food or shelter to the same. The crow, hen-hawk, owl and black bird are not protected by this act. It shall be lawful to shoot robins and black birds on Long Island and Staten Island from the first day of November to the first day of January in each year. (As amended by chapter 641, Laws of 1887.) *English house sparrow and certain other birds excepted from protection; robins, etc., on Long Island.*

Penalty for violations of act. § 7. Any person or persons violating any of the provisions of this act shall be deemed guilty of a misdemeanor, punishable by imprisonment in the county jail or penitentiary, of not less than five or more than thirty days, or to a fine of not less than ten or more than fifty dollars, or both, at the discretion of the court.

Penalties recovered, how applied. § 8. In all actions for the recovery of penalties under this act, one half of the recovery shall belong to the plaintiff, and the remainder shall be paid to the county treasurer of the county where the offense is committed, except if the offense be committed in the city and county of New York, the remaining one-half shall be paid to the chamberlain of said city.

Repeal. § 9. All acts or parts of acts inconsistent with, or contrary to the provisions of this act, are hereby repealed.

(See Laws 1879, Ch. 534.)

CHAPTER 185, LAWS OF 1884.

AN ACT for the better protection of game in Richmond county.

Non-resident not to shoot game without license, etc. SECTION 1. From and after the passage of this act, it shall not be lawful for any non-resident of the county of Richmond to shoot game in any of the towns of said county without having first obtained from a justice of the peace, living in said county, a license for the privilege of so doing. The fee for such license, which shall be good only during the year in which it is granted, shall be ten dollars, and shall be granted as of course by the justice applied to, unless he has proof that the applicant has been convicted of a violation of this act.

§ 2. The money so received by said justices of the peace for such license fees shall be paid by them monthly to the treasurer of said county of Richmond.

§ 3. Any person violating any of the provisions of this act shall, upon conviction, be fined not less than ten nor more than twenty-five dollars.

CHAPTER 485, LAWS OF 1885.

AN ACT relating to game in the counties of Queens and Suffolk.

Unlawful to kill ruffed grouse. SECTION 1. No person shall kill, or have in possession after the same has been killed, in the counties of Queens and Suffolk, any ruffed grouse, commonly called partridge, from the first day of January to the first day of November in each year, under a penalty of twenty-five dollars for each bird or animal so killed or had in possession.

§ 2. No person shall, in said counties, kill or have in possession any bay snipe, sandpiper, shore bird or plover from the first day of January to the tenth day of July in any year, or any rail bird or meadow hen from the first day of January to the first day of September in any year, under a penalty of ten dollars for each bird so killed or had in possession. *Ibid. Bay snipe, plover, etc.*

§ 3. All penalties imposed by this act may be recovered, with costs of suit as fixed by the Code of Civil Procedure, by any person in his own name, or by any incorporated society in its name, before any justice of the peace in the county where the offense was committed, or in any adjoining county, where the amount recovered does not exceed the jurisdiction of said justice, and such penalties may be recovered in the like manner in any court of record in said counties. *Penalties, how recovered.*

§ 4. Any person violating any of the provisions of this act shall be deemed guilty of a misdemeanor, and, upon conviction, shall be punished by a fine of not less than five dollars, or of not more than at the rate of one day for every dollar of the penalty provided by the section so violated, or by imprisonment in the county jail or penitentiary for a period of not less than five days nor more than at the rate of one day for every dollar of any such penalty, or by both such fine and imprisonment in the discretion of the court. *Violation of this act a misdemeanor.*

(See Laws 1879, Ch. 534.)

CHAPTER 247, LAWS 1886.

AN ACT to protect wild goose, duck, brant, teal, coot, dipper and greebe in Chautauqua county.

SECTION 1. No person shall kill, shoot, hunt or pursue any wild goose, duck, brant, teal, coot, dipper or greebe in Chautauqua county between the first day of February and the first day of September in each year. Any person or persons found guilty of violating this act shall be punished by a penalty of twenty-five dollars or thirty days in county jail, or both, as the court may determine. All actions for penalties for violation of this act may be made before a justice of the peace or any court having jurisdiction in Chautauqua county. The money collected under this act shall be divided equally between the poor fund of the county and the person or persons making the complaint.

§ 2. All acts or parts of acts inconsistent with this act are hereby repealed.

(See Laws 1879, Ch. 534.)

CHAPTER 395, LAWS 1886.

AN ACT prohibiting the killing of quail and ruffed grouse, commonly called partridge, within the county of Niagara, for the period of three years from and after the passage of this act.

SECTION 1. No person shall, at any time for the period of three years, from and after the passage of this act, within the county of Niagara, kill, trap or snare any quail or ruffed grouse, commonly called partridge, under a penalty of twenty-five dollars for each quail or ruffed grouse so killed, trapped or snared. Any person offending any of the preceding provisions of this section shall be deemed guilty of a misdemeanor, and shall be prosecuted as directed in section thirty-three of chapter five hundred and thirty-four of the Laws of eighteen hundred and seventy-nine, for the preservation of moose, wild deer, birds, fish and other game, passed June twentieth, eighteen hundred and seventy-nine.

(See Laws 1879, Ch. 534.)

CHAPTER 430, LAWS 1886.

AN ACT for the protection of game in the counties of Chautauqua and Cattaraugus.

Certain game protected. SECTION 1. No person shall ship, transfer or take, without the counties of Chautauqua or Cattaraugus, any ruffed grouse, commonly called partridge, woodcock, snipe or plover, for the purpose of sale or trade, the same having been taken or killed within either of said counties.

Penalty for violations of act. § 2. Any person violating any of the provisions of this act shall be deemed guilty of a misdemeanor, and, upon conviction, shall be punished for each and every bird so shipped, transferred or taken without the bounds of said counties for the purpose of sale or trade, by a fine of not less than twenty-five dollars nor more than one hundred dollar, or by imprisonment in the county jail or penitentiary for a period of not less than twenty-five days nor more than at the rate of one day for every dollar of any such penalty, or by both such fine and imprisonment in the discretion of the court.

Penalties, how recovered. § 3 All penalties imposed by this act may be recovered with costs of suit, as fixed by the Code of Civil Procedure, by any person in his own name, or by any incorporated society in its name, before any justice of the peace in said county, or in any adjoining county where

the amount recovered does not exceed the jurisdiction of said justice, and such penalties may be recovered in like manner in any court of record in said county.
(See Laws 1879, Ch. 534.)

CHAPTER 542, LAWS 1886.

AN ACT in relation to the shooting of quail upon Robins Island.

SECTION 1. The shooting of quail upon Robins Island, in the county of Suffolk, so long as such island remains the property of the Robins Island Club, shall be permitted to be done by the members of that club and their guests on and after the fifteenth day of October in each year, and until the first day of February in the year following.
(See Laws 1879, Ch. 534.)

CHAPTER 416, LAWS 1881.

AN ACT to exempt the waters of Otsego lake from the provisions of sections eighteen, twenty and twenty-three of chapter five hundred and thirty-four, of the Laws of eighteen hundred and seventy-nine, entitled "An act for the preservation of moose, wild deer, birds, fish and other game, and from the provisions of said section twenty-three as amended by chapter four hundred and thirty-one of the Laws of eighteen hundred and eighty— repealing section eight of chapter four hundred and thirty-one of the Laws of eighteen hundred and eighty — and for the protection and preservation of fish in the waters of Otsego lake."

SECTION 1. The waters of Otsego lake, in the county of Otsego, are hereby excepted from the provisions of sections eighteen, twenty and twenty-three of chapter five hundred and thirty-four of the Laws of eighteen hundred and seventy-nine, and from the provisions of said section twenty-three as amended by section one of chapter five hundred and thirty-one of the Laws of eighteen hundred and eighty. *Otsego lake excempted from act named.*

§ 2. Section eight of chapter five hundred and thirty-one of the Laws of eighteen hundred and eighty is hereby repealed.

§ 3. Until the board of supervisors of the county of Otsego shall, under and in pursuance of section thirty-seven of chapter five hundred and thirty-four of the Laws of eighteen hundred and seventy-nine, make provisions for the protection and preservation and regulating the taking of fish from the waters of said Otsego lake, no person shall kill or catch, or attempt to take, kill or catch any fish in the waters *Taking fish except by hook and line prohibited until supervisors act.*

Penalty. of Otsego lake in any manner or with any device except angling with hook and line held in hand. Any person violating the provisions of this section shall be deemed guilty of a misdemeanor, and, in addition thereto, shall be liable to pay a penalty of one hundred dollars for each and every offense, to be recovered as provided in section thirty-three of chapter five hundred and thirty-four of the Laws of eighteen hundred and seventy-nine, and as provided in chapter five hundred and thirty-one of the Laws of eighteen hundred and eighty.

(See Laws 1879, Ch. 534.)

CHAPTER 410, LAWS OF 1882. (CONSOLIDATION ACT.)

Song birds and certain others, when not to be killed. SECTION 2025. No person shall kill, wound, trap, net, snare, catch with bird lime, or with any similar substance or drug, or in any other manner capture or sell, expose for sale, or transport during the months of April, May, June, July, August, September or October, in any year any bird of song, or any linnet, blue-bird, yellow-hammer, yellow-bird, thrush, woodpecker, cat-bird, pewee, swallow, martin, blue-jay, oriole, kildee, snow-bird, grass-bird, grossbeak, phoebe-bird, humming-bird, blackbird, wren, excepting birds bred in a cage or imported from Europe or the southern United States. No person shall kill or expose for sale, or have in his possession after the same has been killed, any robbin, meadow-lark, or starling, between the first day of January and the fifteenth day of October, save only when such birds are killed on the premises of the person killing, and while they are

Exceptions. destroying fruit. This section shall not apply to any person who shall kill any bird for the purpose of studying its habits or history,

Penalty. or having the same stuffed and set up as a specimen. Any person violating this section shall be deemed guilty of a misdemeanor, punishable by imprisonment in the county jail or penitentiary, of not less than five or more than thirty days, and shall also be liable to a penalty of fifty dollars, to be recovered with costs, by any person suing there-

Penalties, how distributed. for in his own name. In all actions for the recovery of penalties under this section, one-half of the recovery shall belong to the plaintiff, and the remainder shall be paid to the chamberlain.

Issue of warrants of arrest in action under game law. § 1306. Any justice of a district court upon receiving sufficient security for costs on the part of the complainant, and sufficient proof by affidavit that any of the provisions of chapter five hundred and thirty-four of the Laws of eighteen hundred and seventy-nine, entitled "An act for the preservation of moose, wild deer, birds, fish and other game," have been violated by any person being tempo-

OF THE STATE OF NEW YORK. 39

rarily within its jurisdiction, but not residing there permanently, or by any person whose name and residence are unknown, is hereby authorized to issue his warrant for the arrest of such offender, and to cause him to be committed or held to bail to answer the charge against him; and any such justice, upon receiving proof or probable cause for believing in the concealment of any game or fish mentioned in said act, and taken during any of the periods prohibited, and upon the complainants giving security, to be approved by such magistrate, for the damage which the defendant in the case may sustain in consequence of the complaint, provided he shall be found not to have violated the law, shall issue his search warrant, and cause search to be made in any house, market, boat, car, or other building, and for that end may cause any apartment, chest, box, locker, crate or basket to be broken open and the contents examined. _{Search warrants.}

FISH.

CHAPTER 498, LAWS 1887.

AN ACT authorizing possession and sale in the city of New York of salmon-trout and certain other varieties of fish taken from waters outside of this State.

SECTION 1. It shall be lawful to have in possession and to sell within the city of New York, at any time, salmon-trout sometimes known as lake trout, also the large mouthed black bass of North Carolina and Virginia locally known as chub, and pike perch, sometimes known as wall-eyed pike, said varieties of fish to be lawfully taken from waters outside of this State. _{Sale in New York city of fish taken outside of the State.}

§ 2. None of the provisions of laws heretofore enacted for the preservation of fish or other game within this State shall be construed to prohibit or interfere with the possession or sale in the city of New York only, of the above specified fish taken from the waters outside of this State, provided that it be proven in any action or prosecution for such possession or sale, that such fish was lawfully taken from waters outside of this State. _{Game laws, how to be construed.}

CHAPTER 530, LAWS 1887.

AN ACT for the protection and preservation of salmon in the waters of this State.

PASSED June 6, 1887; three-fifths being present.

Salmon, catching of, by angling.
SECTION 1. No person shall at any time kill or catch, or attempt to kill or catch, salmon in the waters of this State with any device or in any manner, save that of angling with line or rod held in hand.

Period, limited.
§ 2. No person shall catch, or attempt to catch or kill, any salmon in said waters save only from the first of March to the fifteeenth day of August in each year.

Salmon caught in net to be restored to water.
§ 3. Any person using nets in that part of the Hudson river within the jurisdiction of this State, in fishing for other fish allowed to be taken therein by nets, shall upon catching any salmon immediately return and restore the same to the water without injury. The fore-

Reservation.
going provisions are not to apply to the operations of State or public hatcheries or to the artificial propagation of said fish by State or public authority.

Violations a misdemeanor; how punished.
Actions, how brought.
§ 4. Any person violating any of the foregoing provisions of this act shall be deemed guilty of a misdemeanor, and, in addition, shall be liable to a penalty of one hundred dollars, or one day's imprisonment for each dollar of fine; any informer to receive one-half of said fine. Actions for any violations of this act may be brought before any justice of the peace in any county which borders on the river or water opposite where the offense was committed without regard to channel boundaries.

Repeal.
§ 5. All acts inconsistent with this act are hereby repealed.

CHAPTER 247, LAWS 1884.

AN ACT for the preservation of fish in the Hudson river.

Fishing with a seine prohibited.
SECTION 1. No person shall draw or use any seine, or catch or kill any fish by means of any seine in any of the waters of the Hudson river contained, between any trestle or bank of any railroad running along said river and the adjacent bank of said river. And any person violating any of the provisions of this section shall be deemed guilty of a misdemeanor.

OF THE STATE OF NEW YORK.

CHAPTER 522, LAWS 1886.

AN ACT to prohibit the use of pound nets and purse nets in the Hudson river, between the first day of June and the fifteenth day of October.

SECTION 1. No pound net or purse net shall be used or set in the waters of the Hudson river, from the first day of June until the fifteenth day of October in each and every year.

§ 2. Any person violating the provisions of this act shall be deemed guilty of a misdemeanor.

(See Laws 1879, Ch. 534.)

CHAPTER 226 LAWS 1886.

AN ACT to regulate fishing in the town of Saugerties, Ulster county.

SECTION 1. Any person having in his or her possession on the shores, banks or waters of the Esopus creek, in the town of Saugerties, above the dam at the village of Saugerties, or the shores, banks or waters of any lake or stream of water in said town of Saugerties, other than the Hudson river and the Esopus creek below the dam, at said village of Saugerties, at any time, any snare net, set-line, fike, pot or other devices of an kind used in taking fish, except hook and line held in the hand or attached to fishing rods, shall be deemed guilty of a misdemeanor, and in addition thereto shall be liable to a penalty of twenty-five dollars, to be sued for and recovered by the game constable of said town of Saugerties.

§ 2. The taking of minnows for bait by scap-nets in the Esopus creek proper is not intended to be prohibited by this act.

(See Laws 1879, Ch. 534.)

CHAPTER 407, LAWS 1887.

AN ACT for the preservation and propagation of shad in the Hudson river.

PASSED May 19, 1887.

SECTION 1. No person shall take any shad from the waters of the Hudson river, above the northern boundary line of Westchester county, by means of any seine, net or any other device whatever, from sunset on Saturday to sunrise on the following Monday, between the fifteenth day of March and the fifteenth day of June in each year.

And any such person violating any of the provisions of this section shall be deemed guilty of a misdemeanor, and, in addition thereto, shall be liable to a penalty of fifty dollars for each offense.

Chapter 556, Laws 1885.

An Act to prevent the taking of fish from the waters of Chautauqua lake, by other means than angling.

Fishing by hook and line prohibited. Section 1. No person shall at any time kill in Chautauqua lake, or take from the waters thereof, any fish of any kind, except as taken by the commissioners of fisheries for the purpose of artificial propagation or the stocking of other waters, by any device or means whatever, otherwise than by hook and line.

Unlawful to have trap, net, etc., in possession. § 2. No person shall have in his or her possession, at any time, in or upon the ice or waters of Chautauqua lake any trap or pound net, stake poles, fish house, spear, instrument or device of any kind which may be used for killing or taking fish, except a hook and line.

Penalty. § 3. Any person violating this act shall be guilty of a misdemeanor, and liable to a penalty of fifty dollars for each offense.

Penalties, recovery of. § 4. All penalties imposed by this act may be recovered with costs of suit before any justice of the peace in any town bordering on Chautauqua lake, or in a court of record in Chautauqua county. The district attorney of said county is hereby required to commence action in the name of the people of the State of New York, for the recovery of the penalties hereby allowed, immediately upon receiving proper information of the violation of this act; and any penalty so recovered in a court of record shall be paid to the superintendent of the poor of said county for the benefit of said county poor. One-half of the penalty recovered under this act before any justice of the peace shall belong to the person giving information upon which the action is brought, and the other one-half shall be paid to the supervisor of the town in which the action is brought, for the use of said town. *How disposed of.*

Collection of judgments. All judgments for penalties recovered under this act with the interest thereon, may be collected and payment enforced thereon by execution, and in case of failure to pay the same or any part thereof, the person on whom such penalty is imposed shall be committed to the county jail of said county for a period of not less than ten days, and at the rate of one day for every dollar thereof. Such imprisonment shall not be a satisfaction for such judgment. All charges under this act when made before a justice of the peace shall be a town charge; when in a court of record, a county charge.

§ 5. That portion of chapter four hundred and eighty-two of the Laws of the State of New York, passed eighteen hundred and seventy-five, and chapter one hundred and twenty-two of the Laws of New York, passed eighteen hundred and seventy-eight, and all other acts or parts of acts as are inconsistent and conflicting with this act, relative to the taking of fish from Chautauqua lake, or relative to the powers conferred upon the board of supervisors to regulate such taking of fish from Chautauqua lake, are hereby repealed. *Conflicting acts repealed.*
(See Laws 1875, Ch. 482.)

CHAPTER 395, LAWS 1887.

AN ACT to prohibit catching or killing fish during certain seasons of the year in the county of Steuben.

SECTION 1. It shall be unlawful for any person to catch, kill or expose for sale or have in possession after the same has been caught or killed, any speckled trout, brook trout, or California trout, in the county of Steuben, only from the first day of May to the first day of August in each year. *Catching of trout, season for.*

§ 2. No person shall shoot or spear any fish in the Cohocton river, or any of its tributaries within the county of Steuben, from the first day of April to the first day of July in each year. *Shooting or spearing of fish, when prohibited.*

CHAPTER 603, LAWS 1886.

AN ACT for the better protection of fish in Lake Champlain, its bays and tributaries.

SECTION 1. No person or persons shall catch or kill, or attempt to catch or kill, any fish of any kind in all that part of Lake Champlain, its bays or tributaries, lying or being between the south end of said lake, in the town of Whitehall, Washington county; and Chimney Point, in Essex county, with any set line, seine, gill net, hook net, fyke net, pound net, or net of any kind whatsoever, except for catching minnows for bait, at any time of the year. *Fishing in part of Lake Champlain regulated.*

§ 2. Neither shall any person or persons have in his, her or their possession any muscalonge, black or Oswego bass, pike or pickerel, between the first day of January and the fifteenth day of June in any year. *Possession of certain fish, when prohibited.*

Penalties for violation thereof. § 3. Any person or persons violating any of the provisions of this section, or any of the above sections, shall be guilty of a misdemeanor, and upon conviction thereof shall be subject to a fine of one hundred dollars for each an every net of any kind so used, and in addition thereto shall pay the sum of five dollars for each and every fish caught in any net, or had in possession, contrary to the provisions of this act, or imprisoned in the county jail at hard labor for a period not to exceed one day for each dollar of penalty, with costs imposed.

Penalties, how disposed of. § 4. The above penalties to be paid to the county treasurer of the county in which the offense was committed, and one-half of the above penalties shall be paid by the county treasurer to the complainant on an order from the court before whom the same was tried and adjudged.

Jurisdiction. § 5. Any justice of the peace shall have power and authority to impose fines and imprisonments for violation of any of the above sections, even if said penalty exceed the limits of the justice court.

Powers of game constables. § 6. The game constables elected in either Washington or Essex counties shall have power and authority to arrest, with or without warrant, and bring before the most convenient justice of the peace, in the county where arrested, any person or persons found violating any of the foregoing sections.

(See Laws 1879, Ch. 534.)

Chapter 334, Laws 1886.

An Act to regulate the maintenance and construction of eel weirs in the Oneida river.

Section 1. It shall be lawful to build and maintain in the Oneida river eel weirs of which the lath are not less than one-half an inch apart.

§ 2. All acts and parts of acts inconsistent with the provisions of this act are hereby repealed.

Chapter 141, Laws 1886.

An Act to prevent taking fish from the waters of Lake Ontario adjacent to the shore of Jefferson county, or from the inland waters of said county, by other means than angling.

Fishing in Henderson bay and certain waters prohibited. Section 1. No person shall at any time kill or take from the waters of Henderson bay or Lake Ontario within one mile from the shore between the most westerly point of Pillar Point and the boundary line between the counties of Jefferson and Oswego, or within one mile from the shore of any island in Lake Ontario which is part of Jefferson

OF THE STATE OF NEW YORK. 45

county, except Grenadier Island and Fox Island, or from the waters of any creek, lake or river, or inland waters in the county of Jefferson, any fish of any kind by any device or means whatever, otherwise than by hook and line or rod held in hand. But this section shall not apply to or prohibit the catching of minnows for bait, provided the person using nets for that purpose shall not set them and shall throw back any trout, bass or other game fish taken, and keep only chubs, dace, suckers, or shiners. Proviso.

§ 2. Any person violating any of the provisions of this act shall be guilty of a misdemeanor, and liable to a penalty of fifty dollars for each offense. Penalty.

§ 3. All penalties imposed by this act may be recovered with costs of suit before any justice of the peace or in any court of record in Jefferson county. The district attorney of said county is hereby required to prosecute actions in the name of the people of the State for the recovery of the penalties hereby imposed immediately upon receiving proper information of the incurring of a liability to pay said penalty. Any penalty so recovered in a court of record or before a justice of the peace shall be paid as follows: One-half thereof to the person informing the district attorney, and one-half to the superintendent of the poor of said county, for the benefit of the county poor. All costs or charges incurred in any such prosecutions shall be a county charge. Penalties how recovered.

(See Laws 1879, Ch. 534.)

How applied.

Chapter 366, Laws 1887.

An Act to prevent taking fish from the waters of Lake Ontario adjacent to the shore of Cape Vincent by other means than angling.

Section 1. No person shall at any time kill or take from the waters of Lake Ontario, within one mile from shore between Tibbets Point at the mouth of the St. Lawrence river and the boundary line between the towns of Lyme and Cape Vincent in the county of Jefferson, or within one mile from the shore of Grenadier Island or Fox Island, any fish of any kind by any device or means whatever otherwise than by hook and line or rod held in hand. But this section shall not apply to or prohibit the catching of minnows for bait provided the person using the nets for that purpose shall not set them and shall throw back any trout, bass or other game fish taken, and keep only chubs, dace, suckers or shiners.

Misdemeanor. § 2. Any person violating any of the provisions of this act shall be guilty of a misdemeanor and liable for the penalty of fifty dollars for each offense; which shall be collected in the same manner as provided by section three of chapter one hundred and forty-one of the Laws of eighteen hundred and eighty-six.

Chapter 590, Laws 1886.

An Act to prevent taking fish by net in the waters of the Cattaraugus creek and its mouth.

Net or seine prohibited. Section 1. No person shall set or draw any net or seine in Cattaraugus creek or within eighty rods of its channel into the lake, or take any fish by such means between the fifteenth day of May and the first of November.

Obstructing channel prohibited. § 2. No person shall by any net or device willfully obstruct the channel of said creek so as to prevent the passage of fish therein. Fishing with hook and line permitted in the waters mentioned herein.

Penalty, how recovered. § 3. Any person violating the provisions of this act shall be guilty of a misdemeanor, and, in addition thereto, liable to a penalty of fifty dollars for each offense, to be recovered in the name of the people of this State in any court having jurisdiction thereof. And it shall be the duty of the district attorney of the county in which such offense is committed, on being informed of the fact, to prosecute for the recovery of such penalty, and the recovery after paying the necessary expenses, one-half to be paid to the informer and the other half to the treasurer of the county in which such recovery is had. All acts and parts of acts inconsistent with the provisions of this act are hereby repealed.
(See Laws 1879, Ch. 534.)

Chapter 620, Laws 1887.

An Act to legalize fishing with nets and fykes in certain portions of Cayuga lake, and the outlet of Keuka lake.

Eels, suckers and bullheads, fishing for Section 1. It shall be lawful at any time to fish with nets and fykes and take from the waters of Cayuga lake below Canoga point, about four miles from the foot of said lake, and the outlet of Keuka lake, eels, suckers and bull-heads, but no other kind of fish.

Chapter 547, Laws 1888.

An Act for the better protection of fish in the waters of Richmond county.

Section 1. From and after the passage of this act it shall not be lawful, by day or by night, to put, place, draw, or in any manner use any purse net, pound, weir or other device, except hook and line, for the capture of menhaden or other fish in the waters of Raritan bay, within the jurisdiction of the State of New York and limits of Richmond county, nor in any arm, bay, river, haven, creek, basin, sound or kill thereof. But this act shall not be deemed to prohibit the use of fykes as now allowed by law in accordance with such regulations as the board of supervisors may have declared or may hereafter declare.

§ 2. Any person or persons offending against the provisions of this act shall be deemed guilty of a misdemeanor, and in addition thereto shall be liable to a penalty of one hundred dollars or thirty days' imprisonment, or both, as the court may determine. The money collected under this act shall be divided equally between the poor fund of the county and the person or persons making the complaint.

§ 3. All acts or parts of acts inconsistent with this act are hereby repealed.

Chapter 410, Laws of 1882. (Consolidation Act.)

§ 736. It shall not be lawful except in cases now provided by law, Fish-poles for any person to erect or drive in the soil under water in the harbor of New York, any poles for the purposes of fishing, where the water is of greater depth than six feet in mean low tide, under the penalty of five dollars for each pole erected or driven contrary to the provisions of this section; and it shall be the duty of the board of commissioners of pilots to cause the same to be removed.

§ 737. No person shall fish with seines or any sort of nets, or set Prohibition draws, or raise any seine or net in any part of the channel of the against Hudson river north of Castle Garden, in the city of New York, nets. between the hours of 6 o'clock in the evening and 6 o'clock in the morning. Every person who shall violate any provision of this section Penalty. shall be guilty of a misdemeanor, and shall be punished, on conviction, by imprisonment in a county jail not less than thirty days, or by a fine not less than twenty-five dollars, in the discretion of the court.

§ 738. No person shall set or place, or cause to be set or placed, Obstrucduring the months of March, April or May in any year, in any of the tions at and below New York.

waters of this State at or below the city of New York, any fike-net, gill-net, hoop-net, set-net, or any other net or weir, by means of any hedge, stake, stone, post, pole, anchor or any other fixture to extend into the channel of said waters, or to any greater distance from the shore, in any case, than twenty rods from the ordinary low water mark. Whoever shall violate the provisions of this section shall, for every offense, forfeit the sum of one hundred and fifty dollars for the use of the poor of the county in which such offense shall be committed, to be sued for in the name of the people by the district attorney of any county bordering on the waters on which the offense shall have been committed, to whom notice shall first be given, of the commission of such offense.

Taking of fish in Harlem river and other waters.

§ 739. It shall not be lawful for any person to set or use, for the purpose of taking or capturing fish, a fike or set-net, or other net, in the waters of the Harlem river, or of the East river, or the adjacent waters, or of the confluent brooks within five miles, in any direction from the middle gate, so-called, in said East river, or in any of the adjacent waters or confluent brooks of the main shore and located between the said middle gate and Fort Schuyler, so far as the same are within the county of New York. Any person violating the provisions of this section shall be deemed guilty of a misdemeanor, and shall, on conviction, be subject to a fine of not less than twenty-five dollars or more than one hundred dollars, or imprisonment for not less than ten days or more than thirty days.

Penalty.

Act not to apply to filling in of land under water granted by State, etc.

§ 743. The sections seven hundred and forty and seven hundred and forty-two shall not apply to the depositing of substances upon the building of wharves or piers upon, or the filling in of land under water, granted by the people of the State of New York to any person or persons, provided a permanent and substantial bulkhead be first properly and securely built, inclosing the whole area of any such pier or wharf proposed to be so built or constructed; nor shall such sections apply to the sweeping, washing, or cleaning from the decks of the canal boats, freight, passenger, or pleasure boats, or vessels, of such dirt only as collects naturally thereon from the use thereof by human beings using the same for transportation or pleasure, nor the hauling of fire from the furnace grate of any steamboat having staterooms above the main deck, provided no coal or ashes shall be dumped from the ash box of said steamboat; nor to the setting of shad-poles in the shad season, nor to the use of any other devices or contrivances for the purpose of fishing in any season of the year; but no such setting of shad-poles or devices for fishing shall be allowed below the

Not to sweeping, washing, etc., of boats, etc.

Nor to hauling of fire from furnace grate. Nor to setting shad poles, etc.

OF THE STATE OF NEW YORK. 49

northerly line established by the harbor commissioners of the city of New York; nor shall such sections apply to throwing overboard the refuse and waste matter which ordinarily accumulates in and about canal boats engaged in the transportation of goods and merchandise. But this section shall not be construed to authorize the throwing in said water of food, or any contrivance or device in which food may be kept, carried, or preserved. _{Not to waste matter on canal boats.}

FISH HATCHERIES.

CHAPTER 523 OF THE LAWS OF 1875.

AN ACT making an appropriation for the purpose of restocking the public streams of this State with speckled trout and other fish.

SECTION 1. The sum of fourteen thousand dollars, or so much thereof as shall be necessary, is hereby appropriated out of the general fund to enable the commissioners of fisheries of this State to construct on land, to be purchased therefor, suitable buildings, fixtures and ponds, for the purpose of hatching and rearing speckled trout and other fish, to be used in stocking the public streams of this State with such fish, and to be distributed for the public benefit under such regulations as such commissioners shall prescribe. _{Speckled trout and other fish, hatching, rearing of, appropriation for.}

§ 2. The said commissioners shall account to the comptroller for all expenditures they may make under the provisions of this act.

CHAPTER 320 OF THE LAWS OF 1884.

AN ACT to establish a fish hatchery in the Adirondack forest.

SECTION 1. The commissioners of fisheries are hereby authorized and directed, as soon as possible after the passage of this act, to erect a fish hatching establishment at some convenient point in the Adirondack forest, to be selected by said commissioners, for the purpose of restocking the lakes and streams of said forest with trout and other fish natural to that locality, and stocking such other streams as the commissioners may deem necessary. _{Commissioners to erect fish hatching establishments in the Adirondacks.}

§ 2. The treasurer shall pay to the commissioners of fisheries, upon the warrant of the comptroller, the sum of five thousand dollars, or so much thereof as may be necessary, which sum is hereby appropriated for the purposes of this act. _{$5,000 appropriated}

(See Laws 1885, Ch. 85.)

Chapter 85, Laws 1885.

An Act to grant the use of certain State lands for the purposes of the Adirondack fish hatchery.

Land appropriated

Section 1. The lands belonging to this State, known as lots number four, five and six, in township twenty of great lot number one, Macomb's purchase, in the county of Franklin, on which has been located, pursuant to chapter three hundred and twenty of the laws of eighteen hundred and eighty-four, the Adirondack fish hatchery, are hereby appropriated to the use of such hatchery; but no standing timber shall be cut on such lots except such as shall be needed for building purposes and for fire-wood for such hatchery.

To be in care of commissioners, and fishing prohibited.

§ 2. The lands mentioned in the first section of this act, shall be in the care of the commissioners of fisheries, and no person shall be permitted to fish in the waters of Little Clear pond, nor in its outlet, nor in any other waters on such lands, nor to enter on the same for the purposes of fishing without the consent or by the direction of the commissioners of fisheries; but the said waters shall be held by the said commissioners solely as reservoirs for breeding fish, and nurseries for young fish, and for experimental purposes in the business of fish culture.

Penalty.

§ 3. Whoever shall violate any of the provisions of the second section of this act shall forfeit a penalty of fifty dollars for each offense, to be sued for and recovered with costs of suit, by the said commissioners, in any court of competent jurisdiction in the county of Franklin, and the penalties recovered shall be paid into the State treasury.

Chapter 613, Laws 1887.

An Act to provide for the erection of a fish hatchery at Cold Spring Harbor, and making an appropriation therefor.

Appropriation.

Section 1. There shall be appropriated from any funds in the treasury of the State not otherwise appropriated, for new hatchery buildings and improvement of grounds at the Cold Spring Harbor station of the commissioners of fisheries, five thousand dollars, or so much thereof as shall be necessary, to be expended under the direction of the commissioners of fisheries, on vouchers to be approved by the comptroller; but no money shall be paid out of this appropriation till a lease of the lands and water rights now occupied for such

How expended.

OF THE STATE OF NEW YORK. 51

hatchery shall be executed to the State, rent free, from the owner, for such period as the same may be occupied as a public hatchery, which lease, when accepted by the commissioners, shall be filed in the office of the Secretary of State. {Lease of lands, etc., to State without rent.}

CHAPTER 293, LAWS 1887.

AN ACT to establish a fish hatchery in the Adirondack wilderness.

SECTION 1. The commissioners of fisheries are hereby authorized and directed, as soon as possible after the passage of this act, to erect a fish hatching establishment at Mill creek, an inlet of Round lake, Hamilton county, for the purpose of restocking the lakes and streams of said forest with trout and other fish natural to that locality, and stocking such other streams as the commissioners may deem necessary. {Establishment of fish hatcheries.}

§ 2. The treasurer shall pay to the commissioners of fisheries, upon the warrant of the comptroller, the sum of five thousand dollars, or so much thereof as shall be necessary, which sum is hereby appropriated for the purposes of this act. {Appropriation, and how paid.}

SHELL FISH.
CHAPTER 584, LAWS 1887.

AN ACT to promote and protect the cultivation of shell-fish within the waters of this State, for the appointment of an additional commissioner of fisheries; to authorize the grant of franchises for the use of certain lands under water belonging to the State and to make an appropriation therefor.

PASSED June 16, 1887; three-fifths being present.

The People of the State of New York, represented in Senate and Assembly, do enact as follows:

SECTION 1. The commissioners of fisheries, appointed under chapter three hundred and nine, laws of eighteen hundred and seventy-nine, and his successor in office, shall be known as the shell-fish commissioner, and shall finish and complete the survey now being made under his direction of all the lands under the waters of the State suitable for use for the planting and cultivation of shell-fish, and shall make a map thereof as heretofore provided. He shall finish and complete the survey now being made of all the beds of oysters of natural growth located in the waters of the State, and such beds of oysters of natural growth shall be set apart and preserved, and shall not be deemed to {Shell fish commissioner to complete survey and map. Other duties of.}

be included in the lands for which franchises are to be sold under the provisions of this act. Said commissioner shall ascertain the occupants of all lands claimed to be in the possession or occupation of any person or persons, and no grant of lands so occupied or possessed shall be made, except to the actual occupant or possessor thereof; provided that said occupant or possessor, within one year from the passage of this act, shall make application for, and purchase the same.

Applications of occupants for grants.

§ 2. For the further purposes of this act, the governor is hereby authorized to appoint an additional commissioner of fisheries, who shall be a man of experience in oyster culture, and who shall be a resident of Richmond, Queens, Kings or Suffolk counties.

Additional commissioner of fisheries.

§ 3. Immediately after the passage of this act the commissioners of fisheries shall meet at some place, to be designated by them, in the city of New York, for the purpose of making such rules and regulations as shall be deemed necessary as preliminary to hearing and granting applications for perpetual franchises for the purpose of shell-fish cultivation on the lands under the waters of this State, mentioned in section one of this act, suitable for planting and cultivation of shell-fish. After such rules and regulations shall have been agreed upon and formulated, the said commissioners of fisheries shall proceed to grant franchises for the purposes of shell-fish cultivation, as hereinafter provided. But no such franchise shall be granted until one month's notice of the application for a franchise or franchises shall have been given by posting in a conspicuous place, in the office of the shell-fish commissioner, and in the office of the town clerk of the town nearest to the lands applied for.

Commissioners of fisheries to make rules and regulations.

Granting of franchises for shell-fish culture.

Notice of application, how posted.

§ 4. No grant shall be made to any person or persons who have not resided in this State at least one year preceding the date of application, and no grant shall be made to any person, firm or corporation in excess of two hundred and fifty acres, and no person, firm or corporation shall be allowed to hold, at any one time, more than two hundred and fifty acres.

What persons entitled to receive grants.

Limitation of acres.

§ 5. When the conditions precedent to the granting of franchises, mentioned in the foregoing sections, have been complied with, the commissioners of fisheries are hereby empowered, in the name and behalf of the people of the State of New York, to grant, by written instruments under their hands and seals, perpetual franchises for the purposes of shell-fish cultivation in the lands applied for under the waters of this State, for the consideration of not less than one dollar per acre, if the lands are unoccupied and unused, and not less than twenty-five cents per acre if the lands are in present use and occupa-

Granting of perpetual franchises.

Consideration therefor.

OF THE STATE OF NEW YORK. 53

tion, and the right to use and occupy said grounds for said purposes shall be and remain in the said grantee, his legal representatives or successors forever; provided only that the said grantee, his legal representatives or successors shall actually use and occupy the same for the purposes of shell-fish cultivation, and for no other purpose whatever. And the moneys received for the sale of such franchises shall be paid forthwith into the treasury of this State. *Tenure and objects.*

Payment to State treasury.

§ 6. The franchises thus granted shall be deemed to be personal property, and courts of law and of equity shall have power, authority jurisdiction to determine and enforce the rights of persons, firms or corporations thereto as though such franchises were actually personal property owned and possessed by such persons, firms or corporations, and such franchises may be sold, transferred, assigned or conveyed the same as other personal property. Immediately after the receipt of the aforesaid instruments of conveyance, the grantee shall at once cause the grounds therein conveyed to be plainly marked out by stakes, buoys or monuments, which stakes, buoys or monuments shall be continued by said grantee, his legal representatives or successors. *Franchises deemed personal property.*

Transfer thereof.

Grounds to be plainly marked.

§ 7. The said commissioners are hereby authorized to appoint and employ a clerk whose compensation shall not exceed fifteen hundred dollars per annum, which compensation and the necessary expenses for carrying out the provisions of this act shall be paid by the treasurer upon the warrant of the comptroller, to the order of the said commissioners, upon vouchers to be approved by the comptroller. The said clerk shall give a bond, to be approved by the comptroller, in the penal sum of five thousand dollars, for the faithful performance of his duties. *Clerk of commissioners, how paid.*

Official bond of clerk.

§ 8. The provisions of this act shall not be deemed to limit or interfere with the powers of the commissioners of the land office to grant to owners of uplands adjacent to such fisheries any of the lands under the waters of this State as is now provided by law. But in case any grant shall be made by the commissioners of the land office of any land actually occupied and in use under the provisions of this act for the cultivation of shell-fish, such grant by said commissioners of the land office shall be subject to the right of the occupant to occupy such grounds for two years thereafter for the cultivation and removal of the shell-fish there planted. *Right of land commissioners to make water grants not restricted.*

Right to remove shell-fish.

§ 9. This act shall not apply to nor be held to affect in any way lands under water owned, controlled or claimed under colonial patents or legislative grants by any town or towns, person or persons, in the counties of Suffolk, Queens, Kings and Richmond; lands under the *Colonial patents not affected thereby.*

THE FISH AND GAME LAWS

Other exemptions.
waters of Gardiner's and Peconic bays, ceded by the State to the county of Suffolk, pursuant to chapter three hundred and eighty-five of the Laws of eighteen hundred and eighty-five, lands under water in Jamaica bay, lands in the jurisdiction of the town of Hempstead and Jamaica or in the county of Westchester.

Appropriation. How payable.
§ 10. The sum of three thousand dollars, or so much thereof as may be necessary, is hereby appropriated out of any moneys in the treasury not otherwise appropriated, payable by the treasurer on the warrant of the comptroller to the order of the said commissioners for carrying out the provisions of this act, upon vouchers to be approved by the comptroller.

§ 11. This act shall take effect immediately.

CHAPTER 300, LAWS 1886.

AN ACT for the protection of the natural oyster beds located in the waters of the State of New York.

Deposit of certain acids, etc., injurious to oyster culture prohibited
SECTION 1. It shall not be lawful for any person or persons, corporation or corporations, to place, or cause to be placed, in any manner whatsoever, in any waters within the jurisdiction of the State, any sludge acid or other refuse matter, resulting from the manufacture, or process of manufacture, or treatment of crude or refined material from any oil refinery or oil works, any sugar refinery or sugar works, or from any gas house, or building or buildings used for the making of gas, or to deposit in said waters any substance injurious to oyster

Proviso.
culture, provided, however, that nothing in this section shall be held to apply to to any refuse from the manufacture or handling of crude or refined oil and guano made from menhaden or other oil-bearing fish.

Deposit of ashes, garbage, etc., in certain waters prohibited
§ 2. It shall not be lawful to throw or cause to be thrown from any boat, scow or vessel whatsoever, into the waters of Long Island Sound, or into the bays and harbors opening into the same, west of a line drawn from Eaton's Neck, due north to the boundary line between New York State and the State of Connecticut, any cinders, ashes, refuse or garbage.

Penalties of violations of act.
§ 3. Any person or corporations, violating the provisions of either of the foregoing sections of this act shall be adjudged guilty of a misdemeanor.

§ 4. The oyster commissioner is hereby authorized to appoint a person, who shall be known as the State oyster protector, whose duty it shall be to patrol, under the direction of said oyster commissioner, the oyster regions of the State, for the purpose of enforcing the provisions of this act, and, in a general manner, guarding the oyster property of the State. The salary of said protector shall be one thousand dollars per year, and his salary shall be paid in the same manner and he shall be in all respects on the same footing as the game and fish protectors of the State, appointed under chapter five hundred and ninety-one, Laws of eighteen hundred and eighty. Besides his salary the protector shall be allowed his actual traveling and incidental expenses, not to exceed two dollars per day, and the oyster commissioner may, at his discretion, allow the said protector an assistant, who shall be paid at the rate of two dollars and fifty cents per day for the time of actual service.* {State oyster protector, how appointed. His duties and salary. Traveling expenses, etc., how paid. Assistant protectors how paid.}

CHAPTER 385, LAWS 1884.

AN ACT to cede lands under water of Gardiner's and Peconic bays, to Suffolk county, Long Island, for the cultivation of shell-fish.

PASSED, May 28, 1884.

SECTION 1. All the right, title and interest which the people of the State of New York have in and to the lands under water of Gardiner's and Peconic bays in the county of Suffolk, is hereby ceded to said county, for the purposes of oyster culture, to be managed and controlled by the board of supervisors thereof, provided that such lands shall revert to the State when they shall cease to be used for oyster culture, and provided that nothing in this act shall be held to interfere with the right of the commissioners of the land office to grant lands under water in said bays to owners of adjacent uplands for purposes of commerce or of beneficial enjoyment within the existing bulkhead line. {Interest of State, conditionally released to county.}

§ 2. The board of supervisors of Suffolk county shall have power, and it shall be their duty, within thirty days after the passage of this act, to appoint three commissioners of shell-fisheries in the waters of Gardiner's and Peconic bays and the tributaries thereof, in the county of Suffolk. Said commissioners shall be residents of some one or other of the towns lying contiguous to said bays, and at the first appointment thereof one shall be appointed for the term of one year, one for a term of two years, and one for a term of three years; and {Board of supervisors to appoint commissioners of shell fisheries.}

---

* See Laws 1886, chapter 423.

56   THE FISH AND GAME LAWS

annually thereafter one commissioner shall be appointed for a term of three years. Said commissioners when so chosen shall take the usual oath of office and shall give bonds in one hundred dollars each, to the board of supervisors of said county, conditioned for the faithful performance of their official duties; and all moneys received by them for the sale of the lands hereinafter specified shall be paid over by them to the county treasurer of said county.

When commissioners to cause survey and map to be made, etc.

§ 3. Upon the written application of any person of full age who has been an actual resident of Suffolk county for six months next preceding the date of such application, the said commissioners, or a majority of their members, shall cause a survey and map to be made of any land under water of said bays or the tributaries thereof, suitable for planting oysters thereon, as described in such application, and shall take the proper steps to determine whether there is on said land any natural growth of clams such that one person in one day could take three bushels, or a natural shell bed from which shells can be taken in quantities for use in other places; and if there be no such natural growth or shell bed, said commissioners shall sell and convey to said applicant, by warranty deed, all the right, title and interest which the said county of Suffolk shall have in and to said land. Said applications shall not cover more than four acres, nor shall said commissioners sell and convey to any one person less than one or more than four acres; and they shall receive for said land at the rate of one dollar per acre, together with such further sum as may be deemed by the supervisors of said county sufficient to compensate said commissioners for their services and expense in surveying and setting off said lands and in preparing and executing the proper deeds to said applicants; said deeds shall expressly provide and stipulate that the grantee shall, within one year from the date of their execution, plant a specified quantity of oysters on said land, or otherwise the grant shall be void and the land so granted shall revert to the county.

Applications not to cover more than four acres.

Deeds to be recorded.

§ 4. Any and all grantees of land conveyed under this act shall, within three months from the date of their several grants, have the deed recorded in the office of the county clerk of Suffolk county, and thereafter said land so granted shall be held to be real estate in possession of the grantee and shall be subject to taxation as any other real property.

Reference to commissioners to settle disputes.

§ 5. All questions and disputes in regard to ownership, title, buoys, boundaries, ranges, or extent or location of grounds, may be referred to and settled by the said commissioners of shell-fisheries, who may summon before them all the parties in interest and take sworn statement of facts as claimed on either side. From their decision an appeal may be taken to the county judge, whose decision shall be final.

§ 6. Any person willfully disturbing the bottom of the lands so granted, with intent to remove or injure the shell-fish thereon, shall be guilty of a misdemeanor, and on conviction shall, if said disturbance be done in the day time, be punished by a fine not exceeding one hundred dollars and confiscation to the State of the boat and tools so used, or by imprisonment in the county jail for not exceeding three months or by both such fine and imprisonment in the discretion of the court; but if such disturbance shall take place in the night time, or between sunset and sunrise, the penalty shall be a fine of not more than two hundred and fifty dollars and confiscation to the State of the boat and tools so used, or by imprisonment in the county jail for not exceeding six months, or by both such fine and imprisonment in the discretion of the court. *Disturbing bottom of lands, etc., a misdemeanor*

§ 7. Any justice of the peace in either of the said towns bordering on said bays shall have jurisdiction over offenses under this act. *Jurisdiction.*

CHAPTER 549, LAWS 1874.

AN ACT to provide for the planting and protection of oysters in those portions of the Great South bay, lying in the towns of Islip and Babylon in Suffolk county, wherein the taking of clams can not be profitably followed as a business.

PASSED May 22, 1874.

§ 1. It shall be lawful for any inhabitant of either of the towns of Islip or Babylon, in Suffolk county, of full age, and having resided in either of said towns for one year next preceding, by and with the consent of the oyster commissioners hereinafter named, and upon complying with the provisions of this act hereinafter contained, to locate a lot, not to exceed four acres in extent, under the public waters of the Great South bay, in either of said towns where the taking of clams can not be profitably followed as a business, and he shall be entitled to and shall have the exclusive ownership and property in all oysters upon said lot, and the exclusive right to use the said lot for the purposes aforesaid. (Laws 1878, Ch. 142.) *Any inhabitant of Islip or Babylon may locate lot. Ownership of oysters thereon.*

§ 2. For the purpose of ascertaining and determining what portion or portions of said bay may be taken for the purpose of planting oysters as aforesaid, a board of commissioners, consisting of two from the town of Islip and one from the town of Babylon, whose official title shall be *Oyster commissioners to be appointed.*

"Oyster Commissioners," shall be appointed each by the board of town auditors, or a majority of them, of his or their said town respectively.

Terms of office.
The first appointment to be made within twenty days after the passage of this act, and, when so appointed, they shall hold office until the next annual town meeting; and their successors in office shall annually be appointed in the same manner, on the Tuesday immediately preceding every annual town meeting, Such appointment shall be certified in duplicate, in writing, that by Babylon, by said auditors of Babylon, or a majority of them; that by Islip, by said auditors of Islip, or a majority of them; and a copy of said certificate shall be filed with the town clerk of each of said towns, and it shall be the duty of said town clerks respectively, forthwith to notify each person so appointed in his town, of such appointment. (Laws 1878, Ch. 142.)

Official oath.
§ 3. Every person appointed to the office of oyster commissioner, before he enters upon the duties of his office, and within ten days after he shall be notified of his appointment, shall take and subscribe

Bond.
the oath of office prescribed by the constitution and shall execute, in the presence of the supervisor or town clerk of his town, a bond to the supervisor of his town, in the penalty of not less than two hundred dollars, with one or more sufficient sureties to be approved of by such supervisor or town clerk, conditioned for the faithful performance of his duties as such commissioner, which bond shall be filed in the office of such town clerk. (Laws 1878, Ch. 142.)

Refusal to serve.
§ 4. If any person appointed as such commissioner shall not take and subscribe such oath, and file such bond as herein provided, such neglect shall be deemed a refusal to serve.

Vacancy, how filled.
§ 5. If any person appointed to the office of oyster commissioner shall refuse to serve, or shall die or resign or remove out of town, for which he shall have been appointed, or become incapable of serving, before the Tuesday next preceding the next annual town meeting after he shall have been appointed, the said board of town audit rs, of his said town, shall within ten days after the happening of such vacancy supply the same, as hereinbefore provide. (Laws 1878, Ch. 142.)

Commissioners to locate lot.
§ 6. It shall be the duty of said commissioners, or a majority of them, on application of any such inhabitants as aforesaid, and upon notice to all of said commissioners, to attend and examine the lot applied for and ascertain and determine whether the taking of clams can or can not be profitably followed as a business thereon, and if they shall determine that it can not, then and not otherwise they shall locate the lot for him, which shall be clearly marked and defined by means of buoys, stakes or otherwise, as said commissioners, or a

majority of them, shall direct, and in such manner as shall not interfere with net fishing, as a notice to the public that it has been selected for the purposes aforesaid. And it shall be the duty of said commissioners to procure or cause to be made, all surveys and maps which they may deem necessary for defining the portions of said bay which may be allotted for the purposes aforesaid, describing thereon the lots which may be located under this act, and to file copies of all such surveys and maps in the office of the town clerk of each of said towns. On all questions which may arise under this act as to the location of the lots or the boundaries thereof, or the portions of said bay which may be allotted for the purposes aforesaid, the decision of the said commissioners, or a majority of them, shall be final and conclusive. On payment by any such applicant of the expense of locating his lot, which shall be determined by the said commissioners, but shall in no case exceed the sum of ten dollars, and the additional sum of one dollar per acre as yearly rent, they or a majority of them, shall give to such applicant a certificate showing that he has by their consent located a certain lot, and particularly describing said lot, and stating the amount of charges and rental paid therefor, and that the taking of clams can not be profitably followed thereon as a business, and directing in what manner said lots shall be marked and defined, which certificate shall entitle the person named therein to the possession of said lot for the purposes of this act, so long as he shall keep the said lot clearly defined in the manner so directed by said commissioners; but if such person shall neglect to plant his lot with at least one hundred bushels of oysters and shells during the period of one year from the date of his certificate, or shall neglect to pay said yearly rent on or before the first day of April in each and every year, his rights to the possession of the said lot may be terminated at the option of a majority of said commissioners, and in case such right of any person shall be terminated by the decision of said commissioners as aforesaid, a written certificate of such fact shall be made in duplicate, and one of the said certificates shall be filed with each of the town clerks of said towns. A duplicate of every certificate consenting to the location of any lot as aforesaid shall also be filed by said commissioners with each of the said town clerks, who shall enter the name of the person entitled thereto and the sum or sums specified therein in a book, to be procured and kept by them respectively for that purpose. (Laws 1878, Ch. 142.)

Surveys and map.

Decisions as to locations, etc., final.

Expenses of location and yearly rent.

Certificate of location.

When right to possession may be terminated.

Certificate of the fact.

§ 7. Each of said commissioners shall be allowed the sum of five dollars per day for his services actually rendered under this act, the

THE FISH AND GAME LAWS

Compensation of commissioners. — same to be paid only out of the fund received for locating lots pursuant to section six of this act, and shall not receive therefor any additional fees or compensation from any person or persons whomsoever, and each of said commissioners shall at the usual annual

Commissioners to account. — auditors' meeting of said towns account for and pay over all moneys in his hands to the said board of auditors, to wit: The moneys paid in by inhabitants of Babylon to the board of auditors of the town of Babylon, and all moneys paid in by the inhabitants of the town of Islip, to the board of auditors of the town of Islip, and the said respective boards of auditors shall audit the accounts of the said commissioners or commissioner appointed from their town at the same time and in the same manner as those of other town officers, and shall pay all proper charges for services rendered under and by virtue of the provisions of this act out of the moneys so received, and shall pay

Balance to be paid to supervisor. — the balance, if any, to the supervisor of said town, to be credited on its contingent fund. But no fees or salary allowed any commissioner named under this act shall be a charge upon or be paid by either of said towns of Islip or Babylon. (Laws 1878, Ch. 142.)

Interest in lots assignable. — § 8. It shall not be lawful for any person to retain possession of any such lot after he shall cease to be a resident of either of said towns of Islip or Babylon, but he may sell and assign his interest in any such lot to any inhabitant of either of said towns for one year; but no person shall acquire possession of more than one lot, by purchase or otherwise. (Laws 1878, Ch. 142.)

Arrest and bail — § 10. Any person prosecuted for a penalty under this act may be arrested and held to bail in the same manner as upon warrants issued by justices of the peace; and whenever a hearing shall be had for any

Execution — violation of the provisions of this act, execution shall be issued thereon immediately, in the same manner and with like effect as is provided in section one hundred and forty-three, article nine, title four, chapter two, third part of the Revised Statutes, and all the provisions of said section shall apply to executions issued pursuant to the provisions of this act.

Repeal. — § 12. All acts and parts of acts inconsistent with the provisions of this act are hereby repealed.

Terms of present comissioners. — § 13. Upon the appointing of such commissioners and the filing of the certificates thereof, as herein above provided, the term of office of the present oyster commissioners, now acting in the town of Islip, shall cease. (Laws 1878, Ch. 142.)

Proviso. — § 14. The provisions of this act shall not in any way impair the right of the present owners of oyster lots planted pursuant to the provisions of the act hereby amended. (Laws 1878, Ch. 142.)

§ 15. The title of said act is hereby amended so as to read as follows : An act to provide for the planting and protection of oysters in those portions of the Great South bay, lying in the towns of Islip and Babylon, in Suffolk county, wherein the taking of clams can not be profitably followed as a business. (Laws 1878, Ch. 142.)

Amended Laws 1878, chapter 142 ; section 9, repealed Law 1886, chapter 593; section 12, see Laws 1857, chapter 167; section 11, repealed Laws 1878, chapter 142.

CHAPTER 384, LAWS 1879.

AN ACT to regulate the planting of oysters in the public waters of the town of Hempstead, in the county of Queens.

PASSED, May 28, 1879.

SECTION 1. It shall be unlawful for any person to use or occupy any portion of the public lands under water in the town of Hempstead, in the county of Queens, for the purpose of planting oysters thereon, without first having obtained the license so to use and occupy such lands authorized and provided for in and by chapter six hundred and thirty-nine of the laws of eighteen hundred and seventy-one, entitled "An act to regulate the planting of oysters in the public waters in the towns of Jamaica and Hempstead, in Queens county," nor shall license be granted to any person to so use or occupy more than three acres of such lands. *Use or occupation of land without license.*

License.

§ 2. Any person violating any of the provisions of this act shall be guilty of a misdemeanor.* *Misdemeanor.*

CHAPTER 704, LAWS 1881.

AN ACT for the sale of oysters in all the cities and counties of the State of New York, and the better protection of the retail dealers in the same.

SECTION 1. It shall be lawful to sell oysters in the shell, either by count or measure; but all oysters in the shell not sold by actual count shall be sold in a stave measure which shall be uniform in shape and of the following dimensions : The bottom to be sixteen and a half inches across, from inside to inside, and the top to be eighteen inches across, from inside to inside, and twenty-one inches *Oysters, how to be sold.*

Measure. Dimensions, etc.

---

*See Laws 1859, chapter 468.

diagonal from inside chime to top, and such measure shall be even or struck measure, such measure to be inspected and sealed by the sealer of weights and measures in the city or county of the State of New York where said measures are used.

Misdemeanor to sell, except as herein provided.
§ 2. All oysters sold in the shell by measure shall be sold in the stave measure described in section one of this act, and any person or persons who shall sell or offer for sale oysters in the shell by measure in any other than the lawful sealed measure, shall be deemed guilty of a misdemeanor, and shall, upon conviction, be fined a sum not exceeding one hundred dollars for each offense, or imprisoned in the jail of said city or county where such offense is committed, for a term not exceeding sixty days, or both such fine and imprisonment.

Act, how to be construed.
§ 3. But nothing in this act shall be so construed as to effect the shipment of oysters in barrels to Europe.

CHAPTER 203, LAWS 1831.

AN ACT to restrain the taking of oysters in Hudson river.

Prohibition.
SECTION 1. It shall not be lawful for any person, in any way or manner, to take oysters in the Hudson river, north of the county of New York, in the months of May, June, July or August, in any year.

Fines, how disposed of.
§ 3. One-half of the sum which may be recovered under the preceding section of this act, shall be paid to the superintendents of the poor of the county in which the offense is committed, for the use of the poor, the other half shall be for the use of the person who may sue for and recover the same.

Further restrictions.
§ 4. No person shall take any oysters from their beds, in the Hudson river, within the limits aforesaid, for the purpose of conveying them to another State to have them replanted, under a penalty of two hundred and fifty dollars for each offense, to be sued for and recovered in an action of debt, in the name of the superintendents of the poor of the county in which the offense may be committed, for the use of the poor: Any person who may be prosecuted for a violation of this act may be held to bail.*

---

* Probably repealed by Laws 1849, chapter 194, § 4; § 2 repealed Law of 1886, chapter 593, § 1.

OF THE STATE OF NEW YORK. 63

CHAPTER 468, LAWS 1859.

AN ACT in relation to the planting of shell-fish in the waters of Jamaica bay and creeks adjoining, in the county of Queens.

SECTION 1. The owners and lessees of land lying on Jamaica bay and the streams tributary thereto, in the county of Queens, may plant oysters or clams in the waters of said bay or creeks, opposite their respective lands, extending from low-water mark into said bay, not exceeding four rods in width, and in the creeks not exceeding half the width of said creek; but no one person or association shall plant such bed more than one-quarter of a mile long. *Owners or lessees of land may plant shell fish.*

§ 2. Any owner or lessee so planting oysters or clams, shall designate the locality by two or more stakes driven into the bottom at the extreme corner of the bed so planted, and shall, by a suitable monument erected on the adjacent shore, indicate the fact of such planting, but no stake shall be placed so as to interfere in any way with the navigation of said bay or creeks. *Locality to be designated.*

(Section 3 repealed L. 1886, Ch. 539; see L. 1863, Ch. 493; L. 1865, Ch. 343; L. 1866, Ch. 306; L. 1866, Ch. 753; L. 1868, Ch. 734; L. 1871, Ch. 639; L. 1872, Ch. 659; L. 1878, Ch. 302; L. 1879, Ch. 384.)

CHAPTER 493, LAWS 1863.

AN ACT for the protection of the planting of oysters in the towns of Hempstead and Jamaica, county of Queens, New York.

PASSED May 5, 1863.

SECTION 1. It shall be lawful for any person being an inhabitant of the towns of Hempstead or Jamaica, in Queens county, of said State, and having been such for the period of six months, to plant oysters in any of the public waters within either of the said towns; and upon complying with the provisions of this act hereinafter contained, he shall be entitled to, and have the exclusive ownership and property in, all oysters upon the beds where the same were planted, and the exclusive right to use the said beds for the purpose aforesaid. *Inhabitant privileged to plant shell-fish.*

§ 2. Any person being such inhabitant of either of said towns, may use a portion of the land under the public waters within said town, not to exceed two acres in a bed, and on which there is no natural or planted bed of oysters, for the purpose of planting oysters thereon; but to entitle such person to the privileges and comforts of such act, the portion so selected by him shall be clearly marked and defined by means of stakes, or *Each bed not to exceed two acres.*

otherwise, as a notice to the public that it is selected and is occupied for the purpose aforesaid, and no bed shall be so marked and defined until the bed shall be actually planted by said person; and shall not be so planted or held with less than four hundred bushels to the acre, or at the same rate for less than an acre.

<small>Not lawful for other than planter to remove oysters.</small>
§ 3. Any person being an inhabitant of either of said towns as aforesaid, may, upon complying with the provisions of this act, plant oysters on the beds so designated and marked out, and it shall not be lawful for any person other than the one who planted the oysters, and his legal representatives, to take away said oysters, or to disturb said beds either by oystering thereon, or in any other way disturbing said beds, under the penalty hereinafter provided.

§ 4. Any person other than the one who planted the oysters, or his legal representatives, who shall take any oysters from a bed thus marked out and occupied, as above provided, or who shall oyster on the said beds, or in any way disturb the same, shall be liable to a penalty of fifty dollars for each offense, to be recovered by the owner of the oysters, or his legal representative, in any action brought before any justice of the peace of either of said towns, and shall also be guilty of a misdemeanor, and upon conviction shall be punished by a fine of not over one hundred dollars, or imprisonment in the county jail for not more than sixty days, and by both such fine and imprisonment.

<small>Misdemeanor.</small>

<small>Arrest and bail.</small>
§ 5. Any person prosecuted for a penalty under this act, may be arrested and held to bail in the same manner as upon warrants issued by justices of the peace; and whenever a hearing shall be had for any violation of the provisions of this act, execution shall be issued thereon immediately, in the same manner and with like effect as is provided in section one hundred and forty-three, article nine, title four, chapter two, third part of the Revised Statutes; and all the provisions of said section shall apply to execution, issued pursuant to the provisions of this act.

<small>Forfeiture of rights and privileges.</small>
§ 6. Any person entitled to plant oysters by having complied with the provisions of this act, and any such person who shall have abandoned or ceased to use any such land for the purpose intended by this act, for the period of one year, shall forfeit all rights and privileges to use of the same under this act, and any such person who shall remove from the town and cease to be an inhabitant thereof, shall forfeit all rights and privileges acquired by him under this act, after two years of such removal, which period shall be allowed him for the purpose of removing the oysters planted by him, and remaining on said beds at the time of his removal. (See Laws 1859, chap. 408.)

OF THE STATE OF NEW YORK.

CHAPTER 453, LAWS 1880.

AN ACT to regulate the taking of clams and oysters in the waters of the State of New York on the south side of Staten Island.

PASSED May 27, 1880.

SECTION 1. No person shall at any time in the evening or night, between a half an hour after sunset and a half an hour before sunrise, dig up, catch, take away or remove, any clams or oysters, whether of natural growth or planted, from the waters of the State of New York, or the land or ground under such waters, at any point or place on the south side of Staten Island, lying between a line extending due south from the point known as the point of the beach at Great Kills, in the town of Southfield, Richmond county, and a line extending due south-west from Ward's Point, in the town of Westfield, in said Richmond county. *Catching or removing clams or oysters in certain waters prohibited*

§ 2. Every person who shall violate the provisions of this act shall be guilty of a misdemeanor, and upon conviction thereof shall be punished by a fine of not more than one hundred and not less than ten dollars, or by imprisonment in the county jail not less than ten nor more than thirty days. *Penalty.*

§ 3. This act shall take effect immediately.
(See Laws 1886, chap. 404.)

CHAPTER 343, LAWS 1865.

AN ACT for the protection of the planting of oysters in the county of Queens, New York.

PASSED April 8, 1865.

SECTION 1. It shall be lawful for any person, being an inhabitant of the county of Queens, in this State, and having been such for the period of six months, to plant oysters in any of the public waters within said county, except Hempstead harbor, Jamaica and Hempstead bays and Oyster bay harbor; and upon complying with the provisions of this act hereinafter contained, he shall be entitled to and have the exclusive ownership and property in all oysters upon the beds where the same were planted, and the exclusive right to use the said beds for the purpose aforesaid. *Conditions on which inhabitants of Queens county may plant oysters and may become owners of oyster beds in certain public waters.*

§ 2. Any person being such inhabitant of such county may use a portion of the land under the public waters within such county, except in those named in section first of this act, not to exceed three acres in a bed, and on which there is no natural or planted bed of oysters, for *Who may use lands for planting oysters and on what conditions*

the purpose of planting oysters thereon; but to entitle such person or persons to the privilege and comforts of such act, the portion so selected by him shall be clearly marked and defined by means of stakes or otherwise, as a notice to the public that it is selected and occupied for the purpose aforesaid, and shall not be so planted or held with less than fifty bushels to the acre, or at the same rate for less than one acre. If the person entitled to plant oysters by having complied with the provisions of this act, shall not actually occupy the land so staked out by him by planting oysters thereon within six months, he shall forfeit all rights and privileges to the use of the same under this act. (Laws 1886, Ch. 399.)

§ 3. Any person being an inhabitant of said county as aforesaid may, upon complying with the provisions of this act, plant oysters on the beds so designated and marked out. (Laws 1886, Ch. 593.)

Proceedings in case of prosecutions.

§ 5. Any person prosecuted for a penalty under this act, may be arrested and held to bail in the same manner as upon warrants issued by justices of the peace; and whenever a hearing shall be had for any violation of the provisions of this act, execution shall be issued thereon immediately in the same manner and with like effect as is provided in section one hundred and forty-three, article nine, title four, chapter two, third part of the Revised Statutes; and all the provisions of said section shall apply to execution issued pursuant to the provisions of this act.

When abandonment or removal from county shall cause forfeiture of rights under this act.

§ 6. Any person entitled to plant oysters by having complied with the provisions of this act, and any such person who shall have abandoned or ceased to use any such land for the purpose intended by this act, for the period of one year, shall forfeit all rights and privileges to the use of the same under this act; and any such person who shall remove from the county and cease to be an inhabitant thereof, shall forfeit all rights and privileges acquired by him under this act after two years of such removal, which period shall be allowed him for the purpose of removing the oysters planted by him and remaining on said beds at the time of his removal.

§ 8. All acts or parts of acts inconsistent with the provisions of this act, or any portion thereof, are hereby repealed.

§ 9. This act shall take effect immediately.

(By chapter 93, Laws 1870, the provisions of this act are extended to the waters of Jamaica and Hempstead bays. See Laws 1859, chapter 468, and Laws 1864, chapter 574. Amended Laws 1866, chapter 399; Laws 1870, chapter 93. Section 7 partly repealed, Laws 1879, chapter 402. Sections 4 and 7 and part of section 3, repealed Laws 1886, chapter 595.)

OF THE STATE OF NEW YORK. 67

CHAPTER 399, LAWS 1886.

AN ACT to amend an act entitled "An act for the protection of the planting of oysters in the county of Queens, New York," chapter three hundred and forty-three, passed April eighth, eighteen hundred and sixty-five.

PASSED April 5, 1866.

SECTION 1. [Same as section 2, chapter 343, Laws 1866.]

§ 3. The natural growth or bed of oysters in the waters known as Natural Little Neck bay in said county, is hereby defined as being between low-water mark and a distance of five hundred feet therefrom into the waters of said bay towards its centre, beyond which, in the planting of oysters as provided in the first section of this act, the word "natural" in said section shall not apply.

§ 4. Any person who, having planted oysters in pursuance of said Removal act on natural beds of oysters on any grounds under the public waters aforesaid, shall have until the fifteenth day of August, eighteen hundred and sixty-six, to remove said oysters, after which time said person or persons shall cease to have exclusive right or control over said ground or beds of natural growth of oysters, except as provided in section third of this act.

§ 5. This act shall take effect immediately.

(See Laws 1865, chapter 343; amended Laws 1870, chapter 93; § 2 repealed, Laws 1886, chapter 593.)

CHAPTER 306, LAWS 1866.

AN ACT for the protection of the planting of oysters in the towns of Islip and Huntington, county of Suffolk, New York.

PASSED March 31, 1866.

SECTION 1. It shall be lawful for any person being an inhabitant of Who may the towns of Islip or Huntington, in Suffolk couty, State of New York, oysters in and having been such for the period of six months, to plant oysters in South bay. any of the public waters of the Great South Bay, within either of the said towns; and upon complying with the provisions of this act hereinafter contained, he shall be entitled to and have the exclusive ownership and property in all oysters upon the beds where the same were planted, and the exclusive right to use the said beds for the purpose aforesaid.

§ 3. Any person being an inhabitant of either of said towns, as Taking aforesaid, may, upon complying with the provisions of this act, plant oysters by party other than the planter forbidden.

oysters on the beds so designated and marked out, and it shall not be lawful for any person other than the one who planted the oysters and his legal representatives, to take away said oysters, or to disturb said beds either by oystering thereon, or in any other way disturbing said beds, under the penalty hereinafter provided.

When right to plant forfeited.

§ 6. Any person entitled to plant oysters by having complied with the provisions of this act, and any such person who shall have abandoned or ceased to use any such land for the purpose intended by this act, for the period of one year, shall forfeit all rights and privileges to the use of the same under this act; and any such person who shall remove from the town, and cease to be an inhabitant thereof, shall forfeit all rights and privileges acquired by him under this act, after two years of such removal, which period shall be allowed him for the purpose of removing the oysters planted by him, and remaining on said beds at the time of his removal.

§ 7. This act shall take effect immediately.

(See Laws 1869, chapter 468; amended Laws 1872, chapter 666; repealed as to Huntington, Laws 1880, chapter 240; sections 4 and 5 repealed Laws 1886, chapter 593.)

CHAPTER 666, LAWS 1872.

PASSED May 13, 1872.

SECTION 1. Section two of the act entitled "An act for the protection of the planting of oysters in the towns of Islip and Huntington, county of Suffolk," passed March thirty-one, eighteen hundred and sixty-six, is hereby amended so as to read as follows:

Inhabitant of town may use land under water for the purpose of planting oysters.

§ 2. Any person being such inhabitant of either of said towns may use a portion of the land under public waters within said towns, not to exceed two acres, and on which there is no natural or planted bed of oysters or clams, for the purpose of planting oysters thereon; but to entitle such person to the privileges and comforts of such, all the portion so selected by him shall be clearly marked and defined by means of stakes or otherwise, as a notice to the public that it is selected and occupied for the purpose aforesaid; and no bed shall be so marked and defined until the bed shall be actually planted by such person, and shall not be so planted or used with less than four hundred bushels to the acre, or at the same rate for less than an acre.

Oysters planted on natural

§ 2. Any person who shall have planted oysters on any natural growth of clams before the passage of this amendment shall have two

OF THE STATE OF NEW YORK. 69

years from the date of this amendment allowed him to remove the same, and any oysters remaining on such natural growth of clams beyond that time shall become public property. *growth of clams to be removed.*
(See Laws of 1866, chapter 306; repealed as to Huntington, Laws 1880, chapter 240.)

CHAPTER 240, LAWS 1880.

PASSED May 8, 1880.

SECTION 1. Chapter three hundred and six of the laws of eighteen hundred and sixty-six, entitled "An act for the protection of the planting of oysters in the towns of Islip and Huntington, county of Suffolk, New York," and chapter six hundred and sixty-six of the laws of eighteen hundred and seventy-two, amendatory thereof, so far as said acts affect the present town of Huntington, in said county, are hereby repealed. *Chap. 306 Laws of 1866 and chap. 666 Laws of 1872 repealed so far as it affects town of Huntington.*

§ 2. This act shall take effect immediately.

CHAPTER 404, LAWS 1866.

AN ACT for the better protection of the planting of oysters in the waters of Richmond county and of this State surrounding said county, and to regulate oystering and clamming upon beds of natural growth therein.

PASSED April 5, 1866.

§ 5. Actions for any penalty under this act, brought before any justice of the peace, may be commenced by warrant, and the party arrested and held to bail in the same manner as upon warrant issued by justices of the peace (and such process by warrant shall be deemed the commencement of such action), and the same proceedings had as in civil actions commenced by warrant before justices of the peace, and shall be governed by the same rules. And whenever any judgment thereon shall be had, execution shall be issued thereon immediately in the same manner and with the like effect as is provided in section one hundred and twenty-six, article nine, title four, chapter two, third part of the Revised Statutes; and all the provisions of said sections shall apply to executions issued by any justice of the peace pursuant to the provisions of this act. *Actions for penalties.*

§ 8. In the event of any persons violating the provisions of either of the first, second or sixth sections of this act, if the person or persons by said sections authorized to sue for the penalty therein *When sheriff to seize apparatus, etc.*

prescribed shall so elect, in lieu and instead of suing for said penalty in a civil action, said person or persons may make complaint on oath in writing before any justice of the peace of said county of the infraction of the provisions of either of said sections, describing as near as may be the apparatus, boats and implements used in violating such provisions, and it shall thereupon be the duty of the officer to whom such complaint is made, to issue a warrant under his hand commanding the sheriff or any constable of said county to seize, attach, and safely keep all apparatus, implements, boats or other vessels used by any person or persons in violating the provisions of either of the aforesaid sections of this act.

Duty of sheriff.

§ 9. It shall be the duty of the sheriff or constable receiving such process, to seize and take possession of all such apparatus, implements, boats or other vessels used by any person or persons in violating any or either of the provisions of the aforesaid sections of this act, and such sheriff or constable shall forthwith make return thereof to the officer issuing the same, and hold said property in like manner as upon attachment in justices' courts, until such complaint shall be determined and judgment thereon satisfied, and shall give notice to the owner or person in possession of such property when he will return said warrant, together with a copy of said warrant and the complaint upon which it was issued, and also give notice of such return to the complainant.

Answer and hearing.

§ 10. Upon the return of the said warrant, the person or persons charged with such offense, or the owners or persons in possession of the property so seized, may file an answer denying any or all of the allegations in said complaint alleged, and the hearing of said matter, or the trial of the issues thus joined, may be adjourned upon the application of either party, for a period not exceeding ninety days or longer by consent. If upon the hearing of said matter and trial of said issues, it shall appear that an offense has been committed against any of the provisions of the aforesaid section of this act, judgment therein shall be rendered for the penalty prescribed therein, and for the costs of said attachment at similar rates as upon attachments in justices' courts, and if the person or persons owning or claiming the said property so attached, or some one on their behalf, shall not pay the same within ten days after the rendering of said judgment, the property seized shall be sold in the same manner, and upon like notice as personal property under an execution in said courts under an execution to be issued therefor.

When apparatus, etc., to be sold.

§ 11. Upon return being made of the said sale, after satisfying the amount of the judgment and costs, and the costs of said sale, the balance, if any, shall be paid to the owner or owners of the articles seized, or shall be deposited with the treasurer of the county of Richmond to his or their credit. *Balance, after payment of judgment etc.*

§ 12. Upon the return of said warrant, either party may demand, upon paying the fees therefor, a trial by jury, which jury shall be summoned and empaneled in the same manner as juries in courts of justices of the peace; and the attendance of witnesses for either party, and the giving of testimony as a witness in behalf of either the complainant or the claimant of the property seized, may be compelled in the same manner as in courts of justices of the peace, and the trial of the issues shall be conducted in the same manner as in courts of justices of the peace, and the officer issuing such warrant and executing the same shall be entitled to the same fees as are now prescribed for like service in proceedings by attachments in courts of justices of the peace. *Jury trial.*

§ 13. The proceedings by attachment provided for in the five last preceding sections of this act, shall be a bar to any action or prosecution for the penalties prescribed and imposed in the third, fourth and sixth sections of this act. *Attachment to what, a bar.*

§ 15. The act entitled "An act for the better protection of oysters in Richmond county," passed May fourth, eighteen hundred and sixty-four, and all acts and parts of acts inconsistent with the provisions of this act or any part thereof, are hereby repealed.

§ 16. This act shall take effect immediately.

(See Laws 1880, chap. 453; secs. 1, 2, 3, 4, 6, 7 and 14 repealed Laws 1886, chap. 593.)

CHAPTER 234, LAWS 1870.

AN ACT for the preservation of shell-fish in the waters of South bay in Suffolk county.

PASSED April 15, 1870.

SECTION 1. No person shall catch or take any oysters, clams, mussels or shells in the waters of the South bay, in Suffolk county, with a dredge or drag. *Use of dredge or drag prohibited.*

§ 2. No person shall have in his possession or use a dredge or drag in the waters of the South Bay, for the purpose of catching or taking oysters, clams, mussels, shells or any substance growing on the bottom. *Ibid.*

§ 3. No person shall take any oysters, clams, mussels or shells, or any substance growing on the bottom from any public or private bed, *Taking from pri-*

vate beds regulated or in any of the waters of the said South bay, except between sunrise and sunset on any day.

Penalties for violations. § 4. Every person who shall use any dredge, drag, rake or tongs in the waters of the South bay after sunset at evening, and before sunrise in the morning, shall be deemed guilty of a violation of the provisions of the last preceding section. *Possession of drag or dredge to be evidence of intent to use.* When any person or persons shall be found on the waters on the South bay with a drag or dredge in his or their possession, such possession shall be prima facie evidence of an intent to use the same in violation of the provisions of this act.

Time for taking oysters, spawn, etc., regulated. § 5. No person or persons shall catch or take away oysters, spawn or seed oysters in the waters of the South bay after the fifteenth day of June and before the fifteenth day of September in any year.

Repeal. § 9. All acts and parts of acts inconsistent with the foregoing provisions are hereby repealed.

(Section 8 repealed Laws of 1875, chapter 89; sections 6 and 7 repealed Laws 1886, chapter 593.)

Chapter 639, Laws 1871.

An Act to regulate and protect the planting of oysters in the public waters of the towns of Jamaica and Hempstead, in the county of Queens.

Passed April 20, 1871.

Inhabitants may plant oysters. Section 1. It shall be lawful for any person, being an inhabitant of the towns of Jamaica and Hempstead, in the county of Queens, and having been such for the period of one year, to plant oysters, as provided in section second of this act, in any of the public waters within the said towns, and upon complying with the provisions of this act, *To have exclusive property in oysters and use of beds.* he shall be entitled to and have exclusive property and ownership in all oysters upon the beds where the same were planted, and the exclusive right to use the said beds for the purpose aforesaid; and no person other than such inhabitant of the towns of Jamaica and Hempstead shall have the right or privilege of using any portion of the lands under the said public waters for the purpose of planting oysters thereon.

Non-residents to use waters therefor.

Quanty of land under water allowed any inhabitant. How marked and defined. § 2. Any person, being such inhabitant of the towns of Jamaica and Hempstead, may use a portion of the land under the aforesaid public waters, not to exceed three acres, on which there is no planted bed of oysters, for the purpose of planting oysters thereon; but to entitle such person to the privileges and benefits of this act the portion so selected by him shall be clearly marked and defined, by means of

OF THE STATE OF NEW YORK. 73

stakes or otherwise, as a notice to the public that it is selected and is occupied for the purpose aforesaid; and shall not be so planted or held with less than fifty bushels to the acre, or at the same rate for less than one acre. If the person entitled to plant oysters, by having complied with the provisions of this act, shall not actually occupy the land so staked out by him by planting oysters thereon within six months after the granting of the certificate hereinafter mentioned, he shall forfeit all rights and privileges to the use of the same. *Number of bushels to be planted to the acre. Limitation of time for planting and marking.*

§ 3. Before any person shall occupy any lands under the public waters aforesaid, for the purpose of planting oysters under the provisions of this act, he shall prove to the satisfaction of the board of auditors of town accounts of said town, or a majority of them, that the land selected is not a planted bed of oysters, or, if planted, is not so planted by any person other than the applicant, and shall also prove, by at least five reputable residents and freeholders of said town, that he is, and has been for one year preceding, an inhabitant of the town. All the aforesaid proofs shall be taken in writing and signed and sworn to. Such board of auditors, or a majority of them, shall thereupon give to such person a certificate, under their hands, certifying that they are satisfied from such proof that the applicant is and has been for one year preceding an inhabitant of the town, and that the land selected does not contain a planted bed of oysters, or is not planted by any person other than such applicant. Such a certificate and the depositions aforesaid shall thereupon be filed in the town clerk's office, and the certificate shall be evidence of the facts therein contained. *Town auditors to grant certificate of authority upon proof. Certificate how filed.*

§ 4. Any person being an inhabitant of the town as aforesaid, may, upon complying with the provisions of this act, plant oysters upon the beds so designated and marked, and shall pay, for the use of the said land to the supervisor of the town, the annual rent of five dollars for each acre so occupied or staked off. The sums so received in each year shall be appropriated toward the payment of the current annual expenses of said town; and it shall not be lawful for any person other than the one who planted the oysters and his legal representatives, to take said oysters or to disturb said beds either by oystering or clamming thereon, or in any other way, under the penalty hereinafter provided. *Annual rent to town. How applied.*

§ 6. Any person prosecuted for a penalty under the provisions of this act, may be arrested and held to bail in the same manner as upon warrants issued by justices of the peace, and whenever a recovery shall be had for any violation of the provisions of this act, execution *Arrests authorized.*

74 THE FISH AND GAME LAWS

Execution to issue on recovery. shall be issued thereon immediately in the same manner and with the like effect, as is provided in section one hundred and forty-three, article nine, title four, chapter two, third part of the Revised Statutes, third edition; and all the provisions of said section shall apply to executions issued pursuant to the provisions of this act.

Rights to be forfeited after abandonment of beds for one year. § 7. If any person, after having planted oysters in pursuance to the provisions of this act, shall have abandoned or ceased to use the land whereon the same are planted, for the period of one year, he shall forfeit all the rights and privileges to the use of the same under this act; and any such person who shall remove from the town and cease

Also ceasing to be an inhabitant of town to be an inhabitant thereof, shall forfeit all rights and privileges acquired by him under this act, after one year from such removal, which period shall be allowed him for the purpose of removing the oysters planted by him and remaining in the said beds at the time of his removal.

Right of persons to remove oysters heretofore planted. § 8. All persons now having oysters planted in the said public waters, under the provisions of any former act, shall have until the first day of January, one thousand eight hundred and seventy-two, to remove the same, after which time all such persons shall cease to have

Exclusive right, when to cease. exclusive right or control of the lands whereon the same are planted, unless such person or persons again acquires the right to use said lands under the provisions of this act.

Dredging for oysters prohibited. § 9. It shall not be lawful for any persons to dredge for oysters in any of the said waters; any person found dredging shall be guilty of a misdemeanor, and upon conviction shall be punished by a fine of

Penalty. not over one hundred dollars, or imprisonment in the county jail for not more than sixty days, or by both such fine and imprisonment.

§ 10. This act shall take effect immediately.

(See Laws 1859, chap. 468; amended by Laws 1872, chap. 667. See Laws 1879, chap. 384; sec. 5 repealed Laws 1886, chap. 593.)

CHAPTER 667, LAWS 1872.

AN ACT supplemental to an act entitled "An act to regulate and protect the planting of oysters in the public waters of the towns of Jamaica and Hempstead in the county of Queens," passed April twentieth, eighteen hundred and seventy-one.

PASSED May 13, 1872.

Who may plant oysters. SECTION 1. It shall be lawful for any person, being an inhabitant of the towns of Jamaica and Hempstead, in the county of Queens, and having been an inhabitant thereof at least one year, to plant oysters in any part of the public waters of said towns, or either of them; subject however to the provisions of the second section of the act to which this is a supplement.

§ 2. Whenever any inhabitant of either of said towns shall have proved to the board of auditors of such town where the land applied for is situated, that he is entitled to receive the same, by having complied with the provisions of the second section of the act to which this is a supplement, it shall be the duty of said town board of auditors, or a majority of them, and they are hereby required to give to such persons a certificate, as provided for in the third section of the act to which this is a supplement, whether such persons reside in the same town where the land applied for is situated or not ; provided that where any person residing in one of said towns applies for land lying in the other, such application must be made to the board of auditors of the town where such land is situated.

§ 3. All acts or parts of acts inconsistent with this act shall be and the same are hereby repealed.

§ 4. This act shall take effect immediately.

(See Laws 1871, chapter 639.)

CHAPTER 734, LAWS 1868.

AN ACT for the protection of the planting of oysters in the towns of Gravesend and Flatlands, Kings county.

PASSED May 8, 1868.

SECTION 1. It shall be lawful for any inhabitant of the towns of Gravesend and Flatlands, in Kings county, who shall have been such inhabitants for six months immediately preceding, upon complying with the terms of this act, to plant oysters under the public waters within their respective towns, and to have the exclusive property in the oysters so planted, and the exclusive use of such oyster beds. *Inhabitants may plant oysters. To have exclusive property in oysters and use of beds.*

§ 2. The extent of the land under water so to be used by any one person shall not exceed three acres, and shall be distinctly marked out by stakes or otherwise; but such privilege shall not be exercised without the written permit of the justice of the peace and the supervisor of such respective towns, setting forth the locality of such premises sufficiently to distinguish the same, the terms of such privilege, and the person to whom the same is given. Before granting such permit, evidence satisfactory to the officer granting the same shall be furnished that such premises are not a natural bed of oysters, *Extent of land under water allowed and conditions of use. Supervisors and justices to grant permits.*

and that they are not already occupied or used. A copy of such permit, with the accompanying evidence, shall be deposited in the office of the town clerk of the town where such premises are situated; and such copy of the permit may be used as evidence of the facts therein stated. (Laws 1886, chap. 593.)

<small>Copy of permit to be deposited with town clerk</small>

§ 3. Such privilege shall be forfeited by the person receiving such permit, if the same be not actually used for such purposes within six months from the granting of the same, or if the same be abandoned for a period of six months, or if such person shall cease to be an inhabitant of said town, or shall die; but in any such case of the forfeiture of such privilege, the owner of such oysters, or his legal representatives, shall have six months thereafter to remove the oysters already planted in such beds.

<small>In what cases privileges to be deemed forfeited. Rights to remove oysters planted in cases of forfeitures.</small>

(See Laws 1859, chap. 62; sec. 2, partly repealed Laws 1888, chap. 573; Sup. Ct., 1883, People v. Thompson, 30 Hun, 457.)

FISH-WAYS.

Chapter 620, Laws 1881.

An Act to amend section one of chapter two hundred and fifty-two of the Laws of eighteen hundred and eighty, entitled "An act to provide for the construction of fish-ways in the state dams across the Oswego, Oneida and Seneca rivers."

<small>Passed July 8, 1881.</small>

Section 1. Section one of chapter two hundred and fifty-two of the Laws of eighteen hundred and eighty, entitled "An act to provide for the construction of fish-ways in the State dams across the Oswego, Oneida and Seneca rivers," is hereby amended so as to read as follows:

§ 1. It shall be the duty of the superintendent of public works of this State to cause fish-ways to be constructed and maintained in all the State dams across the Oswego, Oneida and Seneca rivers, to permit the passage of all fish endeavoring to migrate to the waters above said dams. The said superintendent of public works shall construct and maintain said fishways in such manner and according to such plans and specifications as the commissioners of fisheries may prescribe, provided the superintendent of public works shall determine that the construction and maintenance of said fish-ways, in such

<small>Superintendent of public works to build fish-ways in State dams across the Oswego, Oneida and Seneca rivers.</small>

OF THE STATE OF NEW YORK. 77

manner and according to such plans and specifications, will in no way interfere with the due and proper management and navigation of the canals, or materially injure the said dams.

§ 2. This act shall take effect immediately.

CHAPTER 308, LAWS 1883.

AN ACT to reappropriate the moneys appropriated by chapter two hundred and fifty-two of the Laws of eighteen hundred and eighty, entitled "An act to provide for the construction of fish-ways in the state dam across the Oswego, Oneida and Seneca rivers."

PASSED April 25, 1883.

SECTION 1. The sum of five thousand dollars, appropriated by chapter two hundred and fifty-two of the Laws of eighteen hundred and eighty, entitled "An act to provide for the construction of fish-ways in the State dams across the Oswego, Oneida and Seneca rivers," not having been expended, or any part thereof, and two years having elapsed since said appropriation, the said sum of five thousand dollars, or so much thereof as may be necessary, is hereby continued, revived and reappropriated, out of any moneys in the treasury not otherwise appropriated, to build and construct said fish-ways, and it shall be the duty of the superintendent of public works to build and construct the same, as provided by chapter two hundred and fifty-two of the Laws of eighteen hundred and eighty. $5,000 reappropriated.

§ 2. This act shall take effect immediately.

CHAPTER 193, LAWS 1886.

AN ACT to provide for the construction of fish-ways in the State dams across the Oswego and Seneca rivers.

SECTION 1. It shall be the duty of the superintendent of public works of this State to cause to be constructed and maintained in proper manner, in all the State dams across the Oswego and Seneca rivers, and in such manner as not to injure said dams, fish-ways at least one foot in depth at the edge of said dams, and of proper width to allow all fish endeavoring to migrate to the waters of said rivers above the dams to pass over the same. The said fish-ways shall be placed at an angle of not more than thirty degrees, and extend entirely to the running water below the dams, and shall be protected Fishways, by whom and how constructed.

on each side by a gunwale of at least one foot in height to confine the waters therein. Said fish-ways shall be constructed under the supervision of the superintendent of public works, upon plans to be approved by the commission of fisheries for the State of New York, and be located at such places in said dams, and built in such manner as shall best serve the purpose therefor, and of such material as said superintendent of public works shall direct.

<small>Plans therefor, how approved.</small>

<small>Appropriation.</small>

§ 2. The sum of three thousand dollars, or so much thereof as shall be necessary, is hereby appropriated out of any moneys in the treasury not otherwise appropriated, to build said fish-ways.

Chapter 202, Laws 1886.

An Act to provide for the construction of fish-ways in the dams across "Little Salmon river," in the town of Mexico, Oswego county, New York.

<small>Superintendent of public works to construct fish-ways. How constructed.</small>

Section 1. It shall be the duty of the superintendent of public works of this State to cause to be constructed and maintained in proper manner, in all the dams across "Little Salmon river," and in such manner as not to injure said dams, fish-ways of suitable depth, and so constructed as to allow all fish endeavoring to migrate to the waters of said river above the dams, to pass over the same. Said fish-ways shall be placed at an angle of not more than thirty degrees and extend entirely to the running water below the dams, and shall be built upon plans to be approved by the commission of fisheries of this State.

<small>Appropriation.</small>

§ 2. The sum of three thousand dollars, or so much thereof as shall be necessary, is hereby appropriated out of any moneys in the treasury not otherwise appropriated to build said fish-ways.

Chapter 544, Laws 1886.

An Act to provide for the construction of a fish-way in the State dam across the Schoharie river at Fort Hunter, Montgomery county, and the Mohawk river at the aqueduct, Schenectady county.

<small>Construction of certain fish-ways.</small>

Section 1. It shall be the duty of the superintendent of public works of this State to cause to be constructed and maintained in the State dam across the Mohawk river, near the aqueduct in Schenectady county, and in the State dam across the Schoharie river near the

village of Fort Hunter in Montgomery county, in such manner as not to impair said dams, a suitable fish-way in each dam, to allow all the fish endeavoring to migrate to the waters of said rivers above such dams to pass over such dams. The said fish-ways shall be constructed under the supervision of the superintendent of public works, and shall be located at such places in said dams and built in such manner and of such materials as he shall direct. *Duty of superintendent of public works.*

§ 2. The sum of two thousand dollars, or so much thereof as may be necessary, is hereby appropriated, out of any moneys in the treasury not otherwise appropriated, to build said fish-ways. *Appropriation.*

Chapter 55, Laws 1875.

An Act to prohibit fishing near any fish-way established by the State.

Section 1. The commissioners of fisheries of this State are hereby required and directed to erect and maintain at a distance of eighty rods from any fish-way established or constructed by the State in any stream or water-course within its boundaries, sign-boards, on which shall be plainly printed or inscribed the words following, to wit: "Eighty rods to the fish-way. All persons are by law prohibited from fishing in this stream between this point and the fish-way;" said sign-boards to be erected on both sides of the stream, above and below the fish-ways. *Sign-boards to be erected. Inscription thereon.*

§ 2. No person shall catch, or attempt to catch, fish with any device whatever, within a distance of eighty rods from any fish-way established or constructed by the State, in any stream or water-course within its boundaries. *Fishing within eighty rods of fish-ways prohibited.*

§ 3. Any person violating the provisions of the second section of this act shall be deemed guilty of a misdemeanor and shall be liable, upon conviction thereof, to a fine not to exceed twenty-five dollars for every offense or be subject to not more than ten days imprisonment in the county jail; said fine to be recovered before any justice of the peace of the county wherein the offense may be committed, who shall issue his warrant for the arrest of the offender upon the complaint of any person duly verified. *Punishment for violation.*

§ 4. Any fine collected by virtue of the provisions of this act, shall be paid to the overseer of the poor of the town in which the offense was committed, to be applied by said overseer to the credit of the poor fund of said town. *Fine, how disposed of.*

(See Laws 1868, chap. 285.)

THE FISH AND GAME LAWS

CHAPTER 512, LAWS 1887.

AN ACT to provide for the construction of a fish-way in the State dam at Troy.

Duty of superintendent of public works as to constructing fish-ways. SECTION 1. The superintendent of public works of this State is hereby authorized to cause to be constructed, maintained and operated in the State dam across the Hudson river at Troy, in such a manner as not to injure the said dam, a fish-way of proper width and depth to allow all fish endeavoring to migrate to the waters of the said river above the dam to pass over the same; such fishway to be placed at an angle of not more than thirty degrees, and extend entirely to the running water below the dam. *Location and manner of construction.* The said fish-way shall be constructed under the supervision of the fish commissioners of this State, and be located at such a place in said dam, and built in such manner and of such materials as said commissioners may direct. *Fish-way, when closed.* It shall be the duty of the superintendent of public works to close the said fish-way whenever the water in said river shall have reached such a level as to in any wise interfere with the use of the surplus waters on either side of said river by the lessees thereof, or to impede canal navigation.

Appropriation. § 2. The sum of eighteen hundred dollars, or so much thereof as may be necessary, is hereby appropriated out of any moneys in the treasury not otherwise appropriated, to build said fish-way, payable by the treasurer on the warrant of the comptroller to the order of said superintendent.

Rights to surplus waters heretofore granted reserved. § 3. Nothing in this act contained shall be so construed as in any way to interfere with or abridge the rights to the surplus waters created by the erection of the State dam aforesaid demised by the people of the State of New York, in and by a certain grant or lease of said surplus waters, made by the people of the State of New York, to the Lansingburg Dry Dock and Hydraulic Company, the second day of January in the year one thousand eight hundred and thirty-two, and in and by a certain grant or lease of said surplus waters made by the people of the State of New York to George Tibbits, the twenty-sixth day of November, in the year one thousand eight hundred and thirty-five, or to interfere with or abridge the use of said surplus waters, or the rights, liberties and privileges granted and demised by said grants or leases.

Repeal of certain acts, etc. § 4. Chapter five hundred and fifty-five of the Laws of eighteen hundred and seventy, entitled "An act to provide for the construction of fish-ways in the State dams at Troy and Fort Miller, and so much of chapter eight hundred and fifty of the laws of eighteen hundred

OF THE STATE OF NEW YORK. 81

and seventy-two, entitled "An act to provide for the construction of fish-ways in the State dams at Troy and Fort Miller, as relates to an appropriation for said dams, are hereby repealed.

§ 5. This act shall take effect immediately.

CHAPTER 501, LAWS OF 1884.

AN ACT to provide for the construction of fish-ways in the State dams across the Oswego and Seneca rivers.

SECTION 1. It shall be the duty of the superintendent of public works of this State to cause to be constructed and maintained in all the State dams across the Oswego and Seneca rivers, in such manner as not to injure the said dams, fish-ways (where not now constructed), at least one foot in depth at the edge of the dams, and of proper width to allow all fish endeavoring to migrate to the waters of said rivers above the dams, to pass over the same. The said fish-ways shall be placed at an angle of not more than thirty degrees and extended entirely to the running water below the dams, and shall be protected on each side by a gunwale of at least one foot in height, to confine the waters therein. The said fish-ways shall be constructed under the supervision of the superintendent of public works, and be located at such places in said dams and built in such manner and of such materials as he shall direct. *Superintendent to construct fish-ways in State dams.*

How to be placed.

§ 2. [Appropriation.]

CHAPTER 212, LAWS 1862.

AN ACT to facilitate the ingress of salmon into Cayuga lake, and for the protection of the same.

PASSED April 12, 1882.

SECTION 1. The owner or owners of each and every dam, whether such owner be an individual, several individuals or the State, made across the Oswego river, or other rivers leading from the Cayuga lake into Lake Ontario, so as to prevent the usual course of the salmon from going up the said rivers into Cayuga lake, shall, on or before the first day of October next, so alter such dam, by making a slope apron in the channel of said river, at least five feet wide, smoothly planked, descending from the top of the dam on an angle of not more than thirty degrees, and extending to the bottom of the river below, with a side plank of at least one foot in width attached to each side of said apron, in such a manner as to confine the water to the channel-way *Alter the dams on or before the first day of October next.*

11

of said apron in its passage over the dam. Each such dam shall be made at least one foot lower at the place where such apron is joined thereto to create a sufficient draft and depth of water on said apron for the free passage of salmon up said river and over said dams to the waters in Cayuga lake.

<small>Penalty for neglect.</small> § 2. The owner or owners of every such dam, who shall refuse or neglect to build and keep in repair an apron, according to the provisions contained in the foregoing section, shall forfeit the sum of one hundred dollars and costs of suit, for every month he or they may so neglect or refuse, and any person feeling himself aggrieved may prosecute therefor in his own name, by action of debt, in any court having cognizance thereof. The one-half of said penalty when so recovered shall be paid to the person prosecuting therefor, and the other half to the commissioners of highways of the town where such recovery shall be had, to be applied in repairing the roads and bridges in such town.

<small>For preservation of fish.</small> § 3. It shall not be lawful for any person to spear, or in any manner catch or destroy any salmon or other fish, while passing up said apron or aprons, or within distance of ten rods thereof, whereby they may be prevented or disturbed from pursuing their usual course up said river. Every person offending against the provisions of this section, shall, for every such offense, forfeit the sum of twenty-five dollars and costs of suit, to be recovered in the same manner and applied in the same way as provided in the last preceding section.

§ 4. All acts and parts of acts, heretofore passed, in relation to dams or obstructions in the rivers above recited in the first section of this act, conflicting with this act, or regulating the fishery in the same, are hereby repealed.

FOREST PRESERVE.

Chapter 283, Laws 1885.

An Act to establish a forest commission, and to define its powers and duties, and for the preservation of forests.

<small>Forest commission to be appointed by Governor, etc.</small> Section 1. There shall be a forest commission which shall consist of three persons, who shall be styled forest commissioners, and who may be removed by the governor for cause. The forest commissioners shall be appointed by the governor, by and with the advice and consent of the senate.

OF THE STATE OF NEW YORK.   83

§ 2. At the first meeting of the forest commissioners they shall divide Terms of office.
themselves by lot, so that the term of one shall expire in two years,
one in four years, and one in six years from the first day of February
next ensuing. Except as to the three terms of office thus determined,
the term of office of a forest commissioner shall be six years, from
the first day of February on which the preceding term expires.

§ 3. During the month of January in the year eighteen hundred and Future appointments.
eighty-eight, and in every second year thereafter, the governor by and
with the advice and consent of the senate shall appoint one forest commissioner. Vacancies that may exist in the office of a forest commissioner after the commencement of a term of office shall be filled by
the governor's appointment, subject to the confirmation of the senate
at its next session for the unexpired portion of the term in which the
vacancy occurs.

§ 4. The forest commissioners shall serve without compensation, To serve without compensation.
except that there shall be paid them their reasonable expenses incurred
in the performance of their official duties.

§ 5. The forest commission shall have power to employ a forest Forest warden, inspectors etc.
warden, forest inspectors, a clerk and all such agents as they may deem
necessary and to fix their compensations, but the expenses and salaries
of such warden, agents, clerk, inspectors and assistants shall not
exceed in the aggregate, with the other expenses of the commission,
the sum therefor appropriated by the legislature.

§ 6. The trustees of public buildings, under chapter three hundred Office for.
and forty-nine laws of eighteen hundred and eighty-three, shall provide rooms for office for the forest commission, with proper furniture,
and fixtures, and with warming and lights.

§ 7. All the lands now owned, or which may hereafter be acquired, Location of forest preserve.
by the State of New York, within the counties of Clinton (excepting
the towns of Altona and Dannemora), Delaware, Essex, Franklin,
Fulton, Hamilton, Herkimer, Lewis, Saratoga, St. Lawrence, Warren,
Washington, Greene, Ulster and Sullivan, shall constitute and be known
as the forest preserve, except all such lands, not wild lands, as have
been, or may hereafter be, acquired by the State of New York upon or
by foreclosure of, or sale pursuant to any mortgage upon lands made
to the commissioners for loaning certain moneys of the United States,
usually called the United States deposit fund; and all such excepted
lands acquired by the State of New York may be sold and conveyed as
provided by law. (Chapter 520, Laws 1888.)

§ 8. The lands now or hereafter constituting the forest preserve To be kept as wild.
shall be forever kept as wild forest lands. They shall not be sold, nor

THE FISH AND GAME LAWS

forest lands. shall they be leased or taken by any person or corporation, public or private.

Powers and duties of commission. § 9. The forest commission shall have the care, custody, control and superintendence of the forest preserve. It shall be the duty of the commission to maintain and protect the forests now on the forest preserve, and to promote as far as practicable, the further growth of forests thereon. It shall also have charge of the public interests of the State with regard to forests and tree planting, and especially with reference to forest fires in every part of the State. It shall have as to all lands now or hereafter included in the forest preserve, but subject to the provisions of this act, all the powers now vested in the commissioners of the land office, and in the comptroller as to such of the said lands as are now owned by the State. The forest commission may from time to time prescribe rules and regulations, and may from time to time, alter or amend the same, affecting the whole or any part of the forest preserve, and for its use, care and administration; but neither such rules or regulations, nor anything herein contained, shall prevent or operate to prevent the free use of any road, stream or water as the same may have been heretofore used or as may be reasonably required in the prosecution of any lawful business.

Officers may arrest offenders without warrant. § 10. The forest warden, forest inspectors, foresters and other persons acting upon the forest preserve under the written employment of the forest warden or of the forest commission may, without warrant, arrest any person found upon the forest preserve violating any of the provisions of this act; but in case of such arrest, the person making the arrest shall forthwith take the person arrested before the nearest magistrate having jurisdiction to issue warrants in such case, and there make, or procure to be made, a complaint in writing, upon which complaint the magistrate shall act as the case may require.

Commission may bring action for injuries, etc. § 11. The forest commission may bring in the name or on behalf of the people of the State of New York, any action to prevent injury to the forest preserve or trespass thereon, to recover damages for such injury or trespass, to recover lands properly forming part of the forest preserve, but occupied or held by persons not entitled thereto, and in all other respects, for the protection and maintenance of the forest preserve, which any owner of lands would be entitled to bring. The forest commission may also maintain in the name or on behalf of the people of the State, an action for the trespass specified in section seventy-four, article fifth, title five, chapter nine, part one of the Revised Statutes, when such trespass is committed upon any lands within the forest preserve. In such action there shall be recoverable the same penalty, and a like execution shall issue, and the defendant be imprisoned thereunder without being entitled to the liberties of the jail, all as provided in sections seventy-four and seventy-six of the said article; and in such action the plaintiff shall be entitled to an order of arrest before judgment, as in the cases mentioned in section five hundred and forty-nine of the Code of Civil Procedure. The trespass herein mentioned shall be deemed to include, in addition to the acts specified in the said section seventy-four, any act of cutting or causing to be cut, or assisting to cut, any tree or timber standing within the forest preserve, or any bark thereon, with intent to remove such tree or timber, or any part thereof, or bark therefrom, from the said forest preserve. With the consent of the attorney-general and the comptroller, the forest commission may employ attorneys and counsel to prosecute any such action, or to defend any action brought against the commission, or any of its members or subordinates, arising out of their or his official conduct with relation to the forest preserve. Any attorney or counsel so employed shall act under the direction of and in the name of the attorney general. Where such attorney or counsel is not so employed, the attorney-general shall prosecute and defend such actions. Attorney and counsel.

§ 12. In an action brought by or at the instance of the forest commission, an injunction, either preliminary or final, shall upon application be granted, restraining any act of trespass, waste or destruction upon the forest preserve. Injunction to be granted.

§ 13. Whenever the State owns or shall own an undivided interest with any person in any lands within the counties mentioned in section eight of this act, or is or shall be in possession of any such lands as joint tenant or tenants in common with any person who has an estate of free hold therein, the attorney-general shall, upon the request of the forest commission, bring an action in the name of the people of the State of New York, for the actual partition of the said lands according to the respective rights of the parties interested therein; and upon the consent in writing of the forest commission, any such person may maintain an action for the actual partition of such lands, according to the respective rights of the parties interested therein, in the same manner as if the State were not entitled to exemption from legal proceedings, service of process in such action upon the attorney-general to be deemed service upon the State. Such actions the proceedings and the judgment therein, and the proceedings under the judgment therein, shall be according to the practice at the time prevailing in actions of partition, and shall have the same Partition of lands held in common by people with individuals.

force and effect as in other actions, except that no costs shall be allowed to the plaintiff in such action, and except that no sale of such lands shall be adjudged therein. The forest commission may without suit, but upon the consent of the comptroller, agree with any person or persons owning lands within the said town, jointly or as tenants in common with the State for the partition of such lands, and upon such agreement and consent the comptroller shall make on behalf of the people of the State any conveyance necessary or proper in such partition, such conveyance to be forthwith recorded as now provided by law as to conveyances made by the commissioners of the land office.

Income. § 14. All income that may hereafter be derived from State forest lands shall be paid over by the forest commissioner to the treasury of the State.

Accounts. § 15. A strict account shall be kept of all receipts and expenses, which account shall be audited by the comptroller, and a general summary thereof shall be reported annually to the legislature.

Report. § 16. The forest commission shall in January of every year, make a written report to the legislature of their proceedings, together with such recommendations of further legislative or official action as they may deem proper.

Supervisor of town protector of lands. To report injuries to district attorney, who shall prosecute offenders. § 17. The supervisor of every town in the State in which wild forest lands belonging to the State are located, except within the counties mentioned in section seven of this act, shall be by virtue of his office the protector of these lands, subject to the instructions he may receive from the forest commission. It shall be his duty to report to the district attorney for prosecution any acts of spoliation or injury that may be done, and it shall be the duty of such district attorney to institute proceedings for the prevention of further trespass, and for the recovery of all damages that may have been committed, with costs of prosecution. The supervisors shall also report their proceedings therein to the forest commission. In towns where the forest commission shall deem it necessary, they may serve a notice upon the supervisor, requiring him to appoint one or more forest guards, and if more than one in a town, the district of each shall be properly defined. The guard so appointed shall have such powers and perform such duties, and receive such pay as the forest commission may determine.

Forest guards.

Measures to awaken interest in schools on subject of forestry. § 18. The forest commission shall take such measures as the department of public instruction, the regents of the university and the forest commission may approve, for awakening an interest in behalf of forestry in the public schools, academies and colleges of the State,

OF THE STATE OF NEW YORK.

and of imparting some degree of elementary instruction upon this subject therein.

§ 19. The forest commission shall, as soon as practicable, prepare tracts or circulars of information, giving plain and concise advice for the care of woodlands upon private lands, and for the starting of new plantations upon lands that have been denuded, exhausted by cultivation, eroded by torrents or injured by fire, or that are sandy, marshy, broken, sterile or waste, and unfit for other use. These publications shall be furnished without cost to any citizen of the State, upon application, and proper measures may be taken for bringing them to the notice of persons who would be benefited by this advice. *Tracts, circulars, etc.*

§ 20. Every supervisor of a town in this State, excepting within the counties mentioned in section seven of this act, shall be *ex officio* fire warden therein. But in towns particularly exposed to damages from forest fires, the supervisor may divide the same into two or more districts, bounded as far as may be by road, streams of water or dividing ridges of land or lot lines; and he may, in writing, appoint one resident citizen in each district as direct fire warden therein. A description of these districts, and the names of the district fire wardens thus appointed, shall be recorded in the office of town clerk. The supervisor may also cause a map of the fire district of his town to be posted in some public place, with the names of the district fire wardens appointed. The cost of such map, not exceeding five dollars, may be made a town charge, and the services of the fire wardens shall also be deemed a town charge and shall not exceed the sum of two dollars per day for the time actually employed. Within the counties mentioned in section seven of this act, such persons shall be fire wardens as may from time to time be appointed by the forest commission. The persons so appointed shall act during the pleasure of the forest commission, and there shall be applicable to them all the provisions of this act with reference to supervisors and district town wardens. Upon the discovery of a forest fire, it shall be the duty of the fire warden of the district, town or county, to take such measures as may be necessary for its extinction. For this purpose he shall have authority to call upon any person in the territory in which he acts for assistance, and any person shall be liable to a fine of not less than five nor more than twenty dollars for refusing to act when so called upon. *Supervisors ex-officio fire wardens. Towns exposed to damage may be divided and one or more fire wardens appointed. Maps, cost of, etc. Fire wardens in counties named, duties of, etc.*

§ 21. The forest commission, the forest warden, the forest inspector, the foresters, and any other person employed by or under the authority of the forest commission, and who may be authorized by the commission to assume such duty, shall, within the counties men- *Powers and duties of officers named in case of fires in woods.*

tioned in section seven of this act, whenever the woods in any such town shall be on fire, perform the duty imposed upon them, and in such case shall have the powers granted to the justices of the peace, the supervisors and the commissioner of highways of such town, by title fourteen of chapter twenty of part one of the Revised Statutes, with reference to the ordering of persons to assist in extinguishing fires or stopping their progress; and any person so ordered by the forest commission, the forest warden, the forest inspectors, the foresters, or any of them, or any other person acting or authorized as aforesaid, who shall refuse or neglect to comply with any such order, shall be liable to the punishment prescribed by the said title.

Action not to be brought for entry.
§ 22. No action for trespass shall be brought by any owner of land for entry made upon his premises by persons going to assist in extinguishing a forest fire, although it may not be upon his land.

Fences may be destroyed, etc.
§ 23. The fire wardens, or the supervisor, where acting in general charge, may cause fences to be destroyed, or furrows to be plowed, to check the running of fires, and, in cases of great danger, back fires may be set along a road or stream, or other line of defense, to clear off the combustible material before an advancing fire.

Supervisor to report fires, etc.
§ 24. The supervisor of every town, of which he is a fire warden as aforesaid, and in which a forest fire of more than one acre in extent has occurred within a year, shall report to the forest commission the extent of the area burned over, to the best of his information, together with the probable amount of property destroyed, specifying the value of timber, as near as may be, and the amount of cord wood, logs, bark or other forest products, and of fencing, bridges, and buildings that have been burned. He shall also make inquiries and report as to the causes of these fires, if they can be ascertained, and as to the measures employed and found most effectual in checking their progress. A consolidated summary of these returns by counties, and of the information as to the same matter, otherwise gathered by the forest commission shall be included in the annual report of the forest commission.

Railroad companies named to cut and burn grass etc.
§ 25. Every railroad company whose road passes through waste or forest lands, or lands liable to be overrun by fires, within this State, shall twice in each year cut and burn off, or remove from its right of way, all grass, brush or other inflammable material, but under proper care, and at times when the fires thus set are not liable to spread beyond control.

Locomotives to be provided
§ 26. All locomotives which shall be run through forest lands shall be provided, within one year from the date of this act, with approved

OF THE STATE OF NEW YORK.

and sufficient arrangements for preventing the escape of fire from their furnace or ash-pan, and netting of steel or iron wire upon their smoke-stack to check the escape of sparks of fire. It shall be the duty of every engineer and fireman employed upon a locomotive, to see that the appliances for the prevention of the escape of fire are in use and applied, as far as it can be reasonably and possibly done. *With arrangements to prevent escape of fire.*

§ 27. No railroad company shall permit its employés to deposit fire, coals or ashes upon their track in the immediate vicinity of woodlands or lands liable to be overrun by fires, and in all cases where any engineer, conductor or trainmen, discovers that fences along the right of way on woodlands adjacent to the railroad are burning, or in danger from fire, it shall be their duty to report the same at their next stopping place, and the person in charge of such station shall take prompt measures for extinguishing such fires. *Fire, coals and ashes not to be deposited in vicinity of woodlands.*

§ 28. In seasons of drought, and especially during the first dry time in the spring, after the snows have gone and before vegetation has revived, railroad companies shall employ a sufficient additional number of trackmen for the prompt extinguishment of fires. And where a forest fire is raging, near the line of their road, they shall concentrate such help and adopt such measures as shall most effectually arrest their progress. *Trackmen in case of drought, etc.*

§ 29. Any railroad company violating the provisions or requirement of this act, shall be liable to a fine of one hundred dollars for each offense. *Penalty.*

§ 30. The forest commission shall, with as little delay as practicable, cause rules for the prevention and suppression of forest fires to be printed for posting in school-houses, inns, saw-mills, and other wood-working establishments, lumber camps, and other places, in such portions of the State as they may deem necessary. Any person maliciously or wantonly defacing or destroying such notices, shall be liable to a fine of five dollars. It shall be the duty of forest agents, supervisors and school trustees, to cause these rules, when received by them, to be properly posted, and replaced when lost or destroyed. *Rules for prevention of forest fires to be printed and posted.*

§ 31. Any person who shall willfully or negligently set fire to, or assist another to set fire to any waste or forest lands belonging to the State or to another person, whereby the said forests are injured or endangered, or who suffers any fire upon his own land to escape or extend beyond the limits thereof, to the injury of the woodlands of another or of the State, shall be liable to a fine of not less than fifty dollars nor more than five hundred dollars, or to imprisonment of not less than thirty days nor more than six months. He shall also be *Willful setting of fires, how punished.*

liable in an action for all damages that may be caused by such fires; such action to be brought in any court of this State having jurisdiction thereof.

$15,000 appropriated. § 32. Fifteen thousand dollars is hereby appropriated out of any moneys in the treasury not otherwise appropriated, for the purposes of this act. And no liabilities shall be incurred by said forest commissioners in excess of this appropriation.

§ 33. This act shall take effect immediately.

See Laws 1886, chap. 280.

Chapter 280, Laws 1886.

An Act to provide for the taxation of forest lands in the counties known as the Forest Preserve.

Passed May 5, 1886.

Assessment of State lands in forest preserve. Section 1. All wild or forest lands belonging to or which may hereafter be acquired by the State within the limits of the forest preserve, as established by chapter two hundred and eighty-three of the Laws of eighteen hundred and eighty-five, shall be assessed and taxed at a like valuation and at a like rate as those at which similar lands of individuals within such counties are assessed and taxed, subject however to the provisions of this act. *Town assessors to file copy of assessment-roll with Comptroller.* On or before August first in every year, the assessors of the town within which the lands so belonging to the State are situated shall file in the office of the comptroller, and in the office of the forest commission, a copy of the assessment-roll of the town, which, in addition to the other matters now required by the law *Additional statement* to be stated therein, shall state and specify which and how much if any of the lands assessed are forest lands, and also and separately which and how much if any of the lands assessed are lands belonging to the State; such statements and specifications to be verified by the oaths of a majority of the said assessors. *Comptroller may correct assessment.* The comptroller shall thereupon and before the first day of September following, and after hearing the assessors and the forest commission, if they or any of them so desire, correct or reduce any assessment of State lands which may in his judgment be in unfair proportion to the remaining assessments of *Approval of Comptroller of assessment before delivery to town.* lands within the town, and shall in other respects approve the assessment and communicate such approval, and no such assessment of State lands shall be valid for any purpose until the amount of the assessment is so approved by the comptroller, and such approval attached and deposited with the assessment-roll of the town and therewith delivered by the assessors of the town to the supervisor of the town, or other officer authorized to receive the same from the assessors. No tax for the erection of a school-house or opening a road shall be imposed upon State lands, unless such erection or opening shall have been first approved in writing by the forest commission. Payments of the taxes which may be imposed according to law and the provisions of this act upon lands so belonging to the State shall in every year be made by the treasurer of the State upon the certificate of the comptroller as to the lawful and just amount of such taxes, by allowing to the treasurer of the county in which any such lands may be situated a credit of the amount of such taxes due upon such lands, upon the amount payable by such county treasurer in such year to the State for State taxes; providing however that no fees shall be allowed by the comptroller to the county treasurers in adjusting their accounts for such portion of the State tax as is so paid. *Proviso as to tax for school-houses, roads, etc. Taxes upon State lands to be paid by State Treasurer. Credit by county treasurers. No fees allowed to treasurers.*

§ 2. This act shall take effect immediately.

CHAPTER 562, LAWS 1887.

AN ACT to establish parks for the propagation of deer and other game upon lands belonging to the State situated in the Catskill regions.

SECTION 1. The forest commission is hereby authorized and directed to set apart tracts of land not exceeding three in number of such size as they may deem proper belonging to the State in the Catskill region, now constituting a part of the forest preserve, for the purpose of breeding deer and wild game. *Deer and wild game, land set apart for.*

§ 2. Said forest commission may establish all proper rules for the protection of said land and game therein. *Rules for protection.*

§ 3. Said commissioners are authorized to purchase and turn out upon such land such deer or other game as they may think proper. *How stocked.*

§ 4. No game shall be killed or pursued, trapped, or in any way destroyed within the limits of said lands so set apart for a period of five years. *Killing of, prohibited.*

§ 5. The sum of five thousand dollars is hereby appropriated to be paid by the Comptroller, at such time and such amount as the commissioners may desire for the purposes of this act, and the commission is authorized to receive private subscriptions and expend the same for such purposes. *Appropriation.*

PENAL CODE.

Public sports.
§ 265. All shooting, hunting, fishing, playing, horse-racing, gaming or other public sports, exercises or shows upon the first day of the week, and all noise disturbing the peace of the day are prohibited. (See section 32 of chapter 534, Laws 1879).

Punishment of Sabbath breaking.
§ 269. Sabbath breaking is a misdemeanor punishable by a fine not less than five dollars and not more than ten dollars, or by imprisonment in a county jail not exceeding five days, or by both; but for a second or other offense, where the parties shall have been previously convicted, it shall be punishable by a fine not less than ten dollars and not more than twenty dollars, and by imprisonment in a county jail not less than five nor more than twenty days. (Laws 1887, Ch. 535.)

Disposing of tainted food.
§ 408. A person who, with intent that the same may be used as food, drink or medicine, sells or offers or exposes for sale any article whatever which to his knowledge is tainted or spoiled, or for any cause unfit to be used as such food, drink or medicine, is guilty of a misdemeanor.

Non-resident taking or planting oysters.
§ 441. A person, who not being at the time an actual inhabitant and resident of this state, plants oysters in the waters of this state, without the consent of the owner of the same, or of the shore, or gathers oysters or other shell-fish from their beds of natural growth, in any such waters on his own account or for his own benefit, or for the benefit of a non-resident employer, is guilty of a misdemeanor, punishable by imprisonment not exceeding six months, or by fine not exceeding one hundred dollars, or both.

Using net or weir unlawfully in Hudson river.
§ 433. A person who uses any net or weir for setting or attaching nets or a pole or other fixtures in any part of the Hudson river, except as permitted by statute, is guilty of a misdemeanor.

Use of certain dredges.
§ 442. A person who uses a dredge or drag operated by steam, or any dredge or drag weighing over thirty pounds for the purpose of catching, or taking oysters or other shell fish from beds of natural growth in the waters of this State is guilty of a misdemeanor. (Chap. 526, Laws 1888.)

§ 640, subd. 8. Unlawfully takes or carries away, or interferes with, or disturbs by any means the oysters or other shell fish of another, legally planted upon the bed of any river, bay, sound or water; or

OF THE STATE OF NEW YORK. 93

removes, pulls up or destroys any stake, designating or marking out the legally planted oyster bed of another; or (Chapter 491, Laws 1888),

§ 640, subd. 10. Kills, wounds or traps any bird, deer, squirrel, rabbit or other animal within the limits of any cemetery or public burying ground, or of any public park or pleasure ground, or removes the young of any such animal, or the eggs of any such bird, from any cemetery, park or pleasure grounds, or exposes for sale or knowingly buys or sells any bird or animal so killed or taken.

Is punishable by imprisonment not exceeding six months, or a fine not exceeding two hundred and fifty dollars, or both.

§ 15. A misdemeanor, when no special punishment is prescribed, is punishable by imprisonment in a penitentiary or county jail for not more than one year, or by a fine of not more than five hundred dollars or both. *Punishment of misdemeanors.*

INDEX.

ACCOUNTS,   PAGE.
   receipts and expenses... 86

ACTIONS,
   certain penalties and costs recovered in courts of record......... 4
   commissioners may institute suit for confiscation of pound weir or net.. 5
   to be prosecuted to determination where they shall be commenced, 6
   certain actions to be commenced by order of fish and game protectors... 6
   protector has power to discontinue................................ 6
   fees, costs, disbursements in certain actions...................... 7
   moneys necessary in certain actions to be advanced by order of district attorney.. 7
   protector bringing suit to receive one-half fines, etc............. 7
   no action shall lie against person who destroys nets, etc., in compliance with law... 9
   in Chautauqua county 35
   how brought.. 40
   in certain counties.. 45
   proceedings in case of prosecution in Queens county............... 66
   for penalties in Richmond county................................. 69
   to be brought before justice of the peace, to be commenced by warrant, arrest and bail in...................................... 69
   proceedings same as civil action.................................. 69
   when sheriff to seize apparatus...............................69, 70
   complaint in... 70
   answer and hearing in.. 70
   when apparatus to be sold.. 70
   balance after payment of judgment................................ 66
   jury trial... 71
   attachment to what a bar... 71
   brought by forest commissioners for injuries..................... 84
   maintained by forest commissioners for trespass.................. 84
   force and effect 85
   for partition of lands maintained, etc........................... 85
   injunction to be granted... 85
   with regard to partition of lands, force and effect.............. 85
   exception 96
   not to be brought for entry...................................... 88
   may be brought in any court of this State........................ 96
   in case of damages for willful setting of fire................... 90

INDEX.

ADIRONDACKS, PAGE.
    stocking in region of... 18
    fish hatcheries to be erected in................................... 49
    fish hatchery to be established in................................. 49
    lands appropriated for fish hatcheries............................. 50
    establishment of fish hatcheries in................................ 51
    appropriation for and how paid..................................... 51
    part of forest preserve.. 83

ALBANY,
    song and small birds... 32

ALDERMEN,
    in city of New York.. 27
    may employ special detectors....................................... 27
    may pay awards... 27
    may raise tax.. 27

ALE WIVES,
    catching with nets in lake Keuka................................... 16

ANATIDÆ,
    defined as " game birds "... 33

ANGLING,
    catching fish by other means in Otsego lake prohibited......... 37, 38
    salmon... 46
    in certain waters in town of Saugerties............................ 41
    taking fish by other means from Chautauqua forbidden............... 42
    in Henderson bay... 44
    in Lake Ontario.. 44
    in Jefferson county.. 45
    in Lake Ontario regulated.. 45
    in Cattaraugus creek regulated..................................... 46
    in Raritan bay regulated... 47

ANNUAL REPORT,
    of forest commission... 88

ANIMALS,
    young exposed for sale in public grounds, etc...................... 93
    buying or selling.. 93
    killed, wounded or trapped in cemetery, etc........................ 93
    young removed from public grounds.................................. 93

APPROPRIATIONS,
    fish and game protectors... 8
    for construction of fishways....................................... 80
    for purposes of forestry... 90
    for purposes of propagation of deer, etc........................... 91

ASSESSMENT,
    approved by comptroller, etc....................................... 90
    of State lands in forest preserve.................................. 90

INDEX. 97

ASSESSMENT — (*Continued*), PAGE.
  comptroller may correct.. 90
  roll to be filed by town assessors....................................... 90
ATTORNEY-GENERAL,
  may furnish from his office legal assistance for protectors......... 8
  chief protector may apply to him for construction of statutes..... 8
  power when no attorney, etc., is employed......................... 85
ATTORNEYS, ETC.,
  to be employed by forest commission................................. 85
AUDITORS,
  of Babylon to appoint oyster commission............................. 58
  of Islip to appoint oyster commission................................ 58
  oyster commissioners to account to.................................. 60
  to receive moneys.. 60
BABYLON,
  any inhabitant of, may locate lot for oyster bed in Great South
    bay 57
  auditors of, to appoint oyster commissioners........................ 58
  not to pay fees or charges allowed commissioners.................. 60
  non-residents.. 60
BASS,
  catching with nets in Lake Keuka..................................... 16
  in St. Lawrence, Clyde, Seneca and Oswego rivers................. 19
  in Ontario, Conesus and Black lakes.................................. 19
  sale of.. 19
  shutting and drawing off waters..................................... 20
  black, possession of, when prohibited............................... 43
  Oswego, possession of, when prohibited.............................. 43
  when caught in Lake Ontario by net.................................. 45
BAY CONSTABLES,
  duties of.. 29
  penalties for failure to act... 29
  powers of.. 29
BAY SNIPE,
  season for, in certain counties...................................... 35
BIRDS,
  protectors may arrest for violation of laws for protection of...... 7, 8
  imported... 32
  caged 32
  for scientific purposes.. 32
  caged and imported excepted... 38
  buying and selling... 93
  killing, wounding or trapping in cemetery, etc...................... 93
BLACK BASS,
  weight and length of... 19
  catching in certain waters... 19

13

BLACK BASS—(*Continued*), PAGE.
 season for, in Lake Erie... 19
 Niagara river... 19
 exposing for sale in Erie county................................... 19
 may be sold at any time when brought from out of the State...... 39

BLACK BIRDS,
 nests not protected.. 14
 season for... 32
 had in possession or exposing for sale............................. 32
 not protected.. 32
 season for, on Long Island and Staten Island 33
 when not to be taken... 38

BLACK LAKE,
 catching bass and muscalonge in.................................... 19
 spearing in.. 21

BLACK SQUIRREL,
 season for... 13

BLUE BIRD,
 season for... 31
 had in possession or exposing for sale............................. 32
 when not to be taken... 38

BLUE JAY,
 season for... 32
 had in possession or exposing for sale............................. 32

BOBOLINK,
 not to be killed... 32
 had in possession or exposing for sale............................. 32

BRANT,
 killing.. 11
 exposing for sale.. 11
 having in possession... 11
 in the waters of Long Island....................................... 11
 on Long Island sound, Gardner's and Peconic bays, Lake Ontario
  and the Hudson river... 12
 shooting out of floating battery, machine or device................ 12
 in Great South bay... 12
 in Peconic bay... 12
 in Shinnecock bay.. 12
 in Lake Ontario.. 12
 in St. Lawrence and Hudson rivers.................................. 12
 killing with swivel or punt gun.................................... 12
 using other device than gun.. 12
 defined as "game birds".. 33
 season for, in Chautauqua county................................... 35

BRANT LAKE,
 catching black bass in... 19

INDEX.

BREEDING FISH,   PAGE.
    certain waters to be used as reservoirs for.... 50

BROOK TROUT,
    (See Trout.)

BROWN TROUT,
    (See Trout.)

BULL-HEADS,
    in Lake George and other waters 19, 20
    in canals... 20
    killing with spear in certain lakes 21

CALIFORNIA TROUT,
    season for 31
    (See Trout.)

CANADA PARTRIDGE (Spruce Grouse),
    netting or snaring, prohibited................................. 14

CANAL BOATS,
    act not to apply to waste matter, from........................... 49

CANANDAIGUA LAKE 31

CAPE VINCENT,
    Taking fish from Lake Ontario regulated 45

CAT-BIRD,
    season for... 32
    had in possession or exposing for sale............................ 32
    when not to be taken.. 38

CATFISH,
    spearing in certain lakes.. 21
    in canals... 26

CATTARAUGUS CREEK,
    certain game protected in... 36
    penalties, how recovered.. 36
    using nets or seines in, regulated................................. 46
    obstructing channel of, prohibited................................. 46
    angling in, regulated.. 46

CAYUGA LAKE,
    Eels, suckers and bull-heads, fishing for 46

CERTIFICATES,
    to collect birds, etc., for scientific purposes....................... 33
    how granted.. 33
    conditions thereof, terms and penalties........................... 33
    certain birds excepted.. 33
    on Long Island... 33

CHAMBERLAIN,
    to receive part of penalty 38
    to give security for costs.. 38

INDEX.

CHAUTAUQUA LAKE,   PAGE.
    fishing except by hook and line forbidden...................... 42
    commissioners of fisheries, excepted.... 42

CHAUTAUQUA COUNTY,
    season for certain game in 35
    penalties, how donated... 35
    certain game protected in, penalties, how recovered 36

CHUBS,
    catching with nets in Lake Keuka................................. 16
    may be caught with nets in Lake Ontario 45

(See Black Bass.)

CIRCULARS, ETC.,
    prepared by forest commission...................................... 87

CLAMS,
    in Great South bay 57, 58, 59
    oyster commissioners to control the taking of, in Great South bay, 58
    act to regulate the taking of, on the south side of Staten Island... 65
    penalty for violation... 65
    oysters planted on natural growth bed, to be removed.......... 68, 69
    act to protect the planting of, in and about Richmond county.. 69, 71
    in South bay 71, 72

(See Shell-Fish.)

CLINTON COUNTY,
    location of forest preserve 83

CLYDE RIVER,
    catching bass and muscalonge in 19

COHOCTON RIVER,
    season for shooting and spearing fish.............................. 43

COLD SPRING HARBOR,
    provision for fish hatcheries at.................................... 50
    to be in charge of commissioners of fisheries 50
    lease of land, etc 51

COMMISSIONERS OF FISHERIES,
    duties of, in general... 3
    established 3
    commissioners named.. 4
    terms of office.. 4
    appropriation for expenses... 4
    vacancies to be filled by governor 4
    term extended... 4
    to report yearly the condition of fisheries to Legislature.......... 4
    continued with powers conferred upon them....................... 4
    to receive no salary... 4
    to expend only sums appropriated.................................. 4
    additional member to be appointed from Kings, Queens or Suffolk
        counties 4
    authorized to take fish for propagation 4

INDEX.

COMMISSIONERS OF FISHERIES—(Continued),   PAGE.
    when duty to confiscate pound, weir or nets............ 5
    power to appoint game and fish protectors 5
    protector's bond subject to approval of........................ 5
    chief protector's instruction to subordinate subject to approval of, 6
    to erect sign-boards at State fish-ways......................... 25
    to erect sign-boards at State hatcheries....................... 25
    laws relating to.. 30
    authorized to take fish by any means from Chautauqua lake 42
    to erect fish hatcheries in Adirondacks 49
    to account for expenses to comptroller......................... 49
    to construct hatcheries 49
    to sue in Franklin county for certain offenses 50

COMMISSIONERS OF FISHERIES,
    to have charge of fish hatcheries at Cold Spring Harbor........... 50
    to be in care of Adirondack fish hatcheries..................... 50
    to have charge of Mill Creek fish hatchery 51
    certain appointed, to be shell-fish commissioner................ 51
    granting of franchises for shell-fish culture................... 52
    notice of application, how posted............................... 52
    when to make grants... 52
    granting of perpetual franchises................................ 52
    clerk of commissioners, how paid................................ 58
    to make rules and regulations in regard to shell-fish cultivation... 52
    to grant franchises... 52
    official bond of, required by State............................. 53
    right to make water grants not restricted....................... 53
    right to remove shell-fish...................................... 53
    required to erect sign-boards................................... 79
    inscription on sign-boards...................................... 79

COMMISSIONERS OF SHELL FISHERIES,
    supervisors to appoint in Suffolk county........................ 55
    requisites of... 55
    term of office..55, 56
    bond of... 56
    when to cause survey and map to be made......................... 56
    to settle disputes.. 56
    power to summon witnesses....................................... 56

COMPTROLLER,
    not to pay expenses of protectors without certificate of chief protector 8
    commissioners of fisheries to account to, for expenses.......... 49
    power to correct assessment..................................... 90
    to receive copy of assessment-roll 90
    approval of assessments, etc.................................... 90

CONSTABLE,
    duties of..29, 30
    penalties for failure to act.............................29, 30

INDEX.

CONSTABLE—(Continued),   PAGE.
  powers of... 29, 31
  compensation of.. 29, 31

CONVEYANCE,
  made with regard to partition of land............................ 86

COOTS,
  defined as game birds.. 33
  season for in Chautauqua county................................ 35

COUNSEL,
  may be employed by protectors at certain times............. 5, 6
  to be compensated out of certain fines............................ 7
  to be employed by forest commissions............................ 85

COUNTY TREASURER,
  to pay protector bringing suit one-half fines, etc.................. 7
  to receive fines collected in certain actions....................... 7
  to pay one-half proceeds to State treasury........................ 7
  to pay expenses of suit... 7
  to pay game protectors one-half of fine and penalties............ 26
  to receive part of penalty....................................... 32
  to receive all moneys paid to commissioners of shell fisheries..... 56
  to receive no fees... 91
  to credit taxes.. 91

COURTS,
  having jurisdiction.. 27, 28
  to issue warrants.. 30
  how issued.. 30
  when issued... 30
  against non-residents.. 30
  to issue search warrants....................................... 30
  when to issue warrant in action under game law................. 38
  to issue search warrants in action under game laws.............. 38
  to issue warrants for the arrest of non-residents in actions under
    game law.. 39

COSTS... 32

COTTON'S DAM,
  taking fish from.. 20

CROSS LAKE,
  catching fish in... 20

CROWS,
  nests not protected.. 14
  not protected... 33

CURLEW,
  defined as game birds... 33

DACE,
  may be caught with net in Lake Ontario......................... 45

INDEX. 103

DAMS, PAGE.
    to be altered on or before certain time............................ 81
    how altered, construction of, for ingress of salmon................ 82
    penalty for neglect of owners 82

DEEDS,
    of land in Gardner's and Peconic bays to be recorded............ 56

DEER,
    when may be sold... 28
    appropriation for purposes of propagation, etc........ 91
    land set apart for... 91
    commissioners authorized to stock land with...................... 91
    killing, wounding or trapping in cemetery, etc........... 93
    (See Wild Deer.)

DELAWARE COUNTY,
    hunting wild deer in.. 10
    location of forest preserve... 83

DETECTIVES,
    employment of.. 27

DIPPER,
    season for in Chautauqua county................................. 35

DISTRICT ATTORNEY,
    certain actions to be commenced by, on order of protectors........ 6
    at certain times protectors may retain other counsel.............. 7
    may order money advanced for costs, etc., in certain actions...... 7
    to prosecute actions for penalties.......................... 16, 31
    costs 26
    may discontinue actions without costs............................. 31
    to commence action.. 42
    to prosecute... 45
    authorized to prosecute.................................... 46, 48
    duty to prosecute offenders.. 86

DOGS,
    in private parks... 25

DRINKS,
    tainted, selling or exposing for sale.............................. 92

DROUGHT, ETC.,
    duties of railroad companies, in case of.......................... 89

DUCKS,
    shooting out of floating battery, machine or device............... 12
    on Long Island sound, Gardner's and Peconic bays, Lake Ontario
        and the Hudson river... 12
    river.. 33
    sea.. 33
    defined as game birds... 33
    season for, in Chautauqua county.................................. 35

INDEX.

DUTIES,   PAGE.
    of superintendent of public works as to constructing fish-ways, etc.,   80
    of supervisor of every town   86
    of engineers, conductors, etc., to report fires, etc.   89
    of persons in charge of stations   89
    of engineers and firemen in regard to preventing fires, etc   89

EAGLES,
    kill, expose for sale or have in possession   14

EAST BAY,
    fishing in 20, 21

EAST RIVER,
    taking of fish in, regulated   48

EELS,
    in canals   20
    killing with spear in certain lakes   21
    season for   21
    fishing for, in Cayuga and Keuka lakes   46

EEL WEIRS,
    in Oneida river   44

EGGS,
    taking, forbidden   33
    scientific purposes   33
    removing from public grounds   93

ERIE COUNTY,
    bass, muscalonge and pike exposed for sale   19

ESSEX COUNTY,
    powers of game constables   44
    location of forest preserve   83

ESOPUS CREEK,
    taking of minnows allowed   41
    having nets, etc., in possession at certain places on   41

FEES,
    to treasurer   91

FIKES,
    having in possession on certain shores in Saugerties   41

FINES,
    in certain actions to be paid to county treasurer   7
    to whom paid 27, 30
    how enforced   27
    in New York city   27
    one-half to be paid to game protector 27, 30
    taking oysters from Hudson river   62
    how disposed of   62

INDEX. 105

FINES—(Continued), PAGE.
for violation of fishing regulation..................................... 79
how disposed of... 79
with regard to destroying notices, etc............................... 89

FIRES,
to be reported by supervisor, etc..................................... 88

FIRE WARDENS,
supervisors ex officio.. 87
appointed by supervisors in towns exposed....................... 87
names recorded in office of town clerk............................. 87
in counties named.. 87
duties of... 87
term of office.. 87
authority.. 87
power to destroy fences, etc... 88

FISH,
commissioners authorized to take fish for propagation........... 4
other parties authorized to take fish for propagation............. 4
laws for the protection of, to be enforced by protectors......... 6
protectors may arrest for violation of laws for protection of.... 7, 8
taking from private hatcheries.. 17
in Adirondack region 18
catching in Lake George.. 20
catching in certain lakes.. 20
in canals.. 20
in possession, taken from certain waters........................... 21
may be sold in New York city when brought from out of the State, 39
catching with seine in Hudson river, prohibited................... 40
season for shooting and spearing, Cohocton river................ 43
taking from Henderson bay and portion of Lake Ontario, restricted, 44
taking of, in Hudson and East rivers regulated.................... 48
provision for restocking public streams with...................... 49
certain waters in Adirondacks to be used for experiments...... 50
restocking in Adirondack fish hatcheries with.................... 51
preservation of, in passing dams..................................... 82

FISHERIES,
commissioners to take steps towards improving same............ 3
condition of, to be reported to Legislature by commissioners of
fisheries... 4

FISH-FRY,
taking, transportation or possession of 17
in Adirondack region 18

FISH HATCHERIES,
to be erected in Adirondacks... 49
provisions for the purpose of restocking public streams........ 49
lands in Franklin county appropriated for......................... 50
cutting off standing timber for the purpose of.................... 50

14

INDEX.

FISH HATCHERIES — (*Continued*),　　　　　　　　　　　　PAGE.
   in Adirondacks, to be in care of commissioners of fisheries.... 49, 50
   provision for, at Cold Spring Harbor................................. 50
   to be in charge of commissioners of fisheries..................... 50
   establishment of, at Mill creek...................................... 51
   appropriation for, and how paid..................................... 51

FISHING,
   in certain waters in the Adirondacks regulated...................... 50
   prohibited within eighty rods of fish-ways.......................... 79
   on Sabbath.. 92

FISH-POLES,
   driving in soil under water in New York harbor regulated........... 47

FISH-WAYS,
   sign-boards at.. 25
   fishing within eighty rods of State fish-way prohibited......... 25, 79
   destroying or defacing sign-boards prohibited...................... 25
   across Oswego, Oneida and Seneca rivers...................... 76, 77
   to be built by superintendent of public works...................... 76
   appropriation... 77
   across Oswego and Seneca rivers............................... 77, 78
   by whom constructed.. 77
   plans, how approved.. 78
   across "Little Salmon river".. 78
   by whom constructed.. 78
   appropriation... 78
   across Schoharie and Mohawk rivers............................ 78, 79
   by whom constructed....................................... 78, 79, 81
   appropriation,... 79, 80
   duties of superintendent as to construction........................ 80
   location, etc., of construction..................................... 80
   when closed... 80
   how placed.. 81

FLATLANDS,
   planting of oysters in, protected.............................. 75, 76
   　　　　　　　　　(*See Gravesend.*)

FOOD (TAINTED),
   selling or exposing for sale.. 92

FOREST AGENTS,
   duties as to posting and replacing rules........................... 89

FORESTERS, ETC.,
   duties in case of fire in woods..................................... 87
   power in case of fire with reference to assistance................. 88

FOREST COMMISSIONERS,
   removed by governor.. 82
   appointed by governor.. 82
   future appointments.. 83
   vacancies filled by governor....................................... 83

INDEX.

FOREST COMMISSIONERS — (*Continued*), PAGE.
to serve without compensation 83
office for 83
power of 83
terms of office 83
in case of arrest 84
may bring action for injuries, etc. 84
may maintain action for trespass 84
income 86
charge of public interests of State in regard to trees 84
rules and regulations as to preventing use of road, stream, etc. ... 84
power as to land to be included in forest preserve, same as commissioners of land office, etc. 84
power to arrest offenders 84
in regard to rules and regulations 84
extent of power 84
power and duties of 84
power to employ attorney, etc. 85
partition of lands 85
accounts of 86

FOREST COMMISSION,
to consist of three members 82
power to make agreement with regard to partition of land 86
to make written report 86
to require supervisor to appoint guards 86
to take measures to awaken interest in public schools, etc 86
to prepare tracts, circulars, etc. 87
circulation of, tract, etc 87
duties in case of fire in woods 87
power in case of fire, in reference to assistance 88
to receive report of fires from supervisor 88
with regard to printing, etc., rules for prevention of fires 80
authorized to receive private subscriptions, etc. 91
authorized to stock land 91
to set apart land for deer and wild game 92
to establish rules for protection, etc 91
approval of tax in regard to erection of school-houses, etc 91

FOREST GUARDS,
duties and pay 86
to be appointed by supervisors 86

FOREST INSPECTOR,
duties in case of fire in woods 87
power in case of fire, with reference to assistance 88

FOREST PRESERVE,
counties in, trout season 16, 17
having trout for, in possession 18
location of 83
exceptions 83

FOREST PRESERVE—(Continued),   PAGE.
  certain lands acquired by State excepted................ 83
  lands constituting it to be kept wild...................... 83
  land not to be sold nor leased, etc............................ 83, 84
  care of 84
  assessment of State lands................................... 90

FORESTRY,
  instruction in, with regard to public schools, etc.................. 86
  appropriation for... 92

FOREST WARDENS, ETC.,
  expenses and salaries of.. 83
  duties in case of fire in woods....................................... 87
  power in case of fire, with reference to assistance.................. 88

FRANCHISE,
  of land for shell-fish culture to be granted to occupant............ 52
  application to be made for... 52
  rules and regulations in regard to................................. 52
  notice for application, how posted................................. 52
  what persons entitled to receive.................................... 52
  limitation of acres... 52
  granting of, perpetual... 52
  consideration for... 52
  terms and objects of... 53
  payment to State treasury for....................................... 53
  transfer of... 53
  ground to be plainly marked....................................... 53
  rights of commissioners to make, not restricted................... 53
  colonial patents not affected thereby.............................. 53
  other exemption... 54
  how payable... 54
  deemed personal property... 53

FRANKLIN COUNTY,
  commissioners of fisheries to sue in, for certain offenses.......... 50
  certain lands in, appropriated to fish hatcheries.................. 50
  location of forest preserve.. 83

FRIEND'S LAKE,
  catching bass in... 19

FULTON COUNTY,
  location of forest preserve.. 83

FURNACE GRATES,
  act not to apply to hauling fire from............................... 48

GALLI-MULES,
  defined as game birds.. 33

GALLINÆ,
  defined as game birds.. 33

INDEX.

GAME, PAGE.
    laws for the protection of, to be enforced by protectors.............. 6
    commissioners authorized to stock land with..................... 91
    killing of, within limits, prohibited............................ 91
    protected by rules established by forest commission.............. 91

GAME BIRDS,
    defined... 33

GAME CONSTABLES,
    duties of.. 29, 30, 31
    powers of... 29, 30, 31
    penalties for failure to act................................. 29, 30
    board of supervisors to provide for election of................... 29
    in Kings county.. 29
    term of office of... 29
    how chosen.. 29
    compensation of.. 29, 31
    costs of suit a county charge................................... 46
    To receive one-half penalties recovered...................... 46, 48
    authorized to sue.. 41
    powers of, in Washington and Essex counties.................... 44

GAME FISH,
    catching with nets in Lake Keuka.............................. 16
    when caught in Lake Ontario by net............................ 45

GAME LAWS,
    how to be construed... 39

GAMING,
    on Sabbath... 92

GARDNER'S BAY,
    certain oyster beds in, protected............................... 54
    interest of State to, conditionally released to county............. 55
    restriction to concession of.................................... 55

GREENE COUNTY,
    location of forest preserve..................................... 83

GEESE.
    killing.. 11
    exposing for sale.. 11
    having in possession... 11
    in the waters of Long Island................................... 11
    killing with swivel or punt gun................................. 12
    using other device than gun................................... 12
    in Great South bay.. 12
    in Peconic bay.. 12
    in Shinnecock bay... 12
    in Lake Ontario... 12
    in St. Lawrence and Hudson river.............................. 12
    defined as game birds... 33

INDEX.

GRENADIER ISLAND,   PAGE.
    angling in Lake Ontario near, regulated 45

GRANTS,
    for shell-fish culture... 52
    notice of application for, how posted.............................. 52
    what persons entitled to receive................................... 52
    limitation of acres of... 52
    of perpetual franchise... 52
    consideration therefor... 52
    tenure and objects of 53
    deemed personal property.. 53
    transfer thereof 53
    lands to be plainly marked.. 53
    rights of commissioners of fish, to make, not restricted............ 53
    colonial patents not affected thereby............................... 53
    of surplus waters, rights reserved.... 80

GRAVESEND,
    inhabitant may plant oysters.. 75
    to own property... 75
    extent of bed 75
    permits 75
    copy of to be recorded.. 76
    forfeiture 75

GRAY SQUIRREL,
    season for.. 13
                   (See Squirrel.)

GREAT SOUTH BAY,
    geese in.. 12
    inhabitants of Islip may locate oyster bed in....................... 57
    nets in 23
    oysters in 57, 67

GREAT SODUS BAY,
    fishing in.. 20, 21

GREEBE,
    season for, in Chautauqua county.................................... 35

GRASS BIRD,
    season for... 32
    had in possession or exposing for sale 32

GROSS BEAK,
    season for.. 32
    had in possession or exposing for sale 32
    when not to be taken 38

GROUSE,
    defined as wild bird.. 33

HAMILTON COUNTY,
    location of forest preserve 83

INDEX.

HARE,
	PAGE.
season for	13
killing, exposing for sale or having in possession	13
killing or hunting with ferrets	13

(See Rabbits.)

HARLEM RIVER,
taking of fish in, regulated 48

HATCHERIES (Private),
taking fish, spawn or milt from 17

HATCHERIES (Public),
certain restrictions not to apply to 17
certain act not to apply to 40

HAWKS,
not protected 14

HENDERSON BAY,
fishing in 20, 21
fishing in, restricted 44

HEN-HAWK,
not protected 33

HEMPSTEAD,
certain oyster beds in, protected 54
use or occupation of land without license 61
license for planting oysters in 61
inhabitant may plant oysters and have exclusive ownership 63
inhabitant must not use more than two acres 63
to protect the planting of oysters in 72, 73, 74
planting of oysters regulated 74, 75

(See Jamaica.)

HERKIMER COUNTY,
location of forest preserve 83

HORSE RACING,
on Sabbath 92

HOUNDING,
of wild deer in Delaware and St. Lawrence counties 10
in Queens county 10
in Suffolk county and other counties 10

HUDSON RIVER,
shad not to be taken from except at certain period 4
fishing in 21
fishing with seine prohibited 40
when nets not to be used 41
season for shad in part of 41
use of nets in, regulated 47

HUDSON RIVER—(Continued), PAGE.
season for taking oysters from 62
further restrictions......... 62
setting or attaching net or weir...... 92

HUMMING BIRDS,
season for....................................... 32
had in possession or exposing for sale............. 32
when not to be taken 38

HUNTING,
on Sabbath........... 92

HUNTINGTON,
acts for the protection of planting oysters in.............. 67, 68, 69
repealed 69

(See Islip.)
INCOME,
received by forest commission......... ....:..... 86

INJURIES,
what they include....................................... 85

ISLIP,
any inhabitant of, may locate lot for oyster beds in Great South bay 57
auditor of to appoint oyster commissioner...................... 58
not to pay fees or charges allowed oyster commissioners........... 60
non-resident... 60
inhabitants of town may plant oysters in Great South bay......... 67
taking away oysters by party other than inhabitant............ 67, 68
when right to plant forfeited.. 98
inhabitant may use land to plant................................... 68
oysters planted on natural growth bed of clams........ .... 68, 69

JAMAICA,
inhabitant may plant oysters and have exclusive ownership....... 63
inhabitant not to use more than two acres......................... 63
to protect the planting of oysters in............................. 72
inhabitant may plant oysters...................................... 72
to have exclusive property in beds..... 72
non-residents to use waters in.................................... 72
quantity of land under water allowed any inhabitant............... 72
how marked and defined 72
number of bushels to be planted to the acre....................... 73
limitation of time 73
auditor to grant certificate...................................... 73
how filed.. 73
annual rent...................................... 73
how applied....'''... 73
arrests authorized.. 73
execution to issue on recovery.................................... 74
abandonment................. 74

INDEX. 113

JAMAICA — (Continued), PAGE.
right to recover oysters.. 74
dredging, etc... 74
to regulate the planting of oysters................................ 74
who may plant.. 74
when entitled to bed... 75

JAMAICA BAY,
certain oyster beds protected..................................... 54
owner or lessees of land in, may plant oysters.................... 63
locality for, to be designated..................................... 63

(See Jamaica.)

JEFFERSON COUNTY,
angling in Lake Ontario regulated................................. 45
fishing in waters of, restricted.................................. 45

JUDGMENTS,
how collected... 42

KEUKA LAKE,.. 31
catching minnows in, for bait..................................... 16
eels, suckers and bull-heads, fishing for......................... 46

KILDEE,
season for.. 32
had in possession or exposing for sale............................ 32

KILLING, ETC.,
of game within limits prohibited................................. 91

KINGS COUNTY,
song and small birds.. 32
planting of oysters in, regulated............................ 75, 76

LAKE CHAMPLAIN,
fishing in.. 20, 21
fishing in, regulated.. 43

LAKE CONESUS,
catching bass and muscalonge in.................................. 19

LAKE ERIE,
catching black bass in.. 19

LAKE GEORGE,
season for trout and land-locked salmon........................... 18
catching black bass in.. 19
killing bull-heads... 19
catching pickerel in.. 20
catching fish in.. 20

LAKE HURON,
salmon, trout and land-locked salmon in........................... 20

LAKE MAHOPAC,
catching black bass in.. 19

15

LAKE MICHIGAN,
salmon, trout and land-locked salmon in 20

LAKE ONTARIO,
catching trout through the ice 16
catching trout in, for stocking 17
trout in spawning season... 17
catching bass and muscalonge in............................ 19
catching fish in... 20
fishing in 21
fishing in portions of, restricted................................. 44
taking fish from, by other means than angling, forbidden......... 45

LAKE SUPERIOR,
salmon, trout and land-locked salmon in 20

LAKE ST. CLAIR,
salmon, trout and land-locked salmon in......................... 20

LAKE TROUT,
(See Salmon-Trout.)

LAND,
protected by rules established by forest commission 91

LAND-LOCKED SALMON,
how should be caught... 15, 16
in Lake Ontario, Niagara river, in private waters............. 15, 16
setting net near mouth of Oswego river 16
in Adirondack region 18
from forest preserve in possession 18
season for.. 18
in Lake George.. 18
in certain lakes.. 20

LAND UNDER WATER,
certain restrictions not to apply to.............................. 48
hauling fire from grates.. 48
setting shad-poles.. 48
waste matter on canal boats...................................... 49

LEWIS COUNTY,
location of forest preserve...................................... 83

LICENSES,
to shoot game in Richmond county............................. 34
fee for same... 34
granted by justice; money paid to county treasurer.............. 34

LITTLE CLEAR POND,
fishing in, regulated.. 50

LITTLE NECK BAY,
natural oyster beds in... 69
removal of oysters in.. 69

INDEX. 115

LITTLE SALMON RIVER, PAGE.
fish-way across 78
by whom constructed 78
appropriation 78

LINNET,
season for 31
had in possession 32
exposing for sale 32
when not to be killed 38

LIMICOLÆ,
defined as game birds 33

LOCOMOTIVES,
to be provided with arrangements to prevent escape of fire 88, 89

LONG ISLAND,
season for robins and black birds 33

MENHADEN,
angling for, in Raritan bay, regulated 47

MAP,
of lands under water 51
costs of certain maps 87
of fire district 87
with names of fire wardens 87

MARTIN,
kill, expose for sale or had in possession 14
season for 32
had in possession or exposing for sale 32

MEADOW HEN,
season for, in certain counties 35

MEADOW LARK,
kill, expose for sale or had in possession 14
season for 32
had in possession or exposing for sale 32
not to be killed 32
when not to be killed or had in possession 38

MEDICINE,
selling or exposing for sale tainted 92

MILL CREEK,
establishment of fish hatchery at 51
appropriation for, and how paid 51

MILT,
taking from private hatcheries 17
in Adirondack region 18

INDEX.

MINNOWS,   PAGE.
    catching of, for bait in lake Keuka 16
    catching in certain lakes 20
    in canals 20
    taking of, in Esopus creek not affected by act 41
    not protected when caught for bait in Lake Ontario ... 45

MOHAWK RIVER,
    fish-way across 78, 79
    by whom constructed 78, 89
    appropriation 79

MOOSE,
    protectors may arrest for violation of laws for protection of 7, 8
    hounding of 11
    killing 11
    selling or exposing for sale 11
    having in possession 11

MUD HENS,
    defined as game birds 33

MUD LAKE,
    spearing in 21

MUSCALONGE,
    sale of 19
    catching in certain waters 19
    season for 19
    in Lake Erie and Niagara river 19
    exposing for sale in Erie county 19
    in St. Lawrence, Clyde, Seneca and Oswego rivers ... 19
    in Ontario, Conesus and Black lakes 19
    possession of, when prohibited 43

MUSSELS,
    in South bay 71, 72

NESTS,
    destroy or rob 14
    not to be destroyed 33
    scientific purpose 33

NETS,
    nets, etc., may be destroyed when used in violation of law 9
    in the waters of Lake Ontario 16
    in Oswego river 16
    in Keuka lake 16
    contraband 21
    possession of, on shore 21
    Lake Ontario excepted 22
    Walkill river 22
    may be destroyed when 21
    size of meshes of nets and fykes 22

NETS — (*Continued*),   PAGE.
  in Richmond county... 22
  Long Island.. 22
  menhaden nets... 22
  Lake Ontario 22
  Lake Erie.. 22
  Hudson river... 22, 23
  Coney Island creek.. 22
  for bait 22
  for eel fishing... 23
  in Great South bay.. 23
  for flounder fishing.. 23
  netting song birds and certain others, season for............. 31, 32
  netting song and wild birds....................................... 32
  song and other birds, when not to be caught with.............. 38
  salmon caught in, to be returned to water....................... 40
  when not be used in Hudson river............................... 41
  having in possession on certain shores in Saugerties............ 41
  unlawful to have in possession on Chautauqua lake............. 42
  forbidden in Lake Champlain..................................... 43
  using in Cattaraugus creek regulated............................ 46
  use of, in Hudson river regulated................................ 47
  using in Raritan bay regulated................................... 47
  use of, in New York harbor regulated........................ 47, 48
  using in Hudson and East rivers regulated..................... 48
  setting or attaching 92
              (*See Pound and Weir.*)

NEW YORK CITY,
  warrants of arrest in.. 30
  search warrants in.. 30

NEW YORK COUNTY,
  song and small birds 32

NEW YORK HARBOR,
  fish-poles in, regulated 47
  obstruction in, regulated 47, 48

NIAGARA COUNTY,
  season for certain game suspended 36

NIAGARA RIVER,
  catching trout through the ice.................................... 16
  catching black bass in 19
  catching fish in... 20

NIGHT HAWK,
  kill, expose for sale or had in possession........................ 14

NURSERIES,
  certain waters to be used as 50

OBSTRUCTIONS,
  in New York harbor, regulated.............................. 47, 48

118 INDEX.

ONEIDA LAKE, PAGE.
catching fish in.. 20

ONEIDA RIVER,
eel weir... 44
fish-way across... 76, 77
to be built by superintendent of public works........... 76
appropriation.. 77

ONONDAGA LAKE,
catching fish in.. 20

ORIOLE,
kill, expose for sale or had in possession................. 14
season for... 32
had in possession or exposing for sale................... 32

OSWEGO BASS,
season for... 19
in Lake Erie and Niagara river............................. 19
exposing for sale in Erie county........................... 19

OSWEGO RIVER,
catching bass and muscalonge in......................... 19
fish-way across.. 76, 77, 78
to be built by superintendent of public works........... 76
appropriation.. 77
by whom constructed.. 77
plans, how approved... 78

OTSEGO LAKE,
exempted from certain act.................................. 37

OWLS,
nests not protected... 14
not protected.. 33

OYSTERS,
in Hempstead, county of Queens........................... 61
how to be sold... 61
measure, dimensions, etc.................................... 61
misdemeanor to sell.. 62
shipping to Europe excepted................................ 62
season for, in Hudson river................................. 62
further restrictions... 62
condition on which inhabitants of Queens county may plant oysters
  and become owners of beds in certain public waters............ 65
who may use lands for planting oysters, and on what conditions, 65, 66
lot to be marked and defined................................ 66
proceedings in case of prosecution......................... 66
when abandonment or removal from county shall cause forfeiture
  of rights.. 66
natural beds in Little Neck bay............................. 67
removal of oysters, etc...................................... 67

OYSTERS—(*Continued*),   PAGE.
  act to regulate the taking of, on the south side of Staten Island... 65
  penalty for violation.. 65
  act for planting of, in Queens county....................... 65, 67, 68
  in South bay... 71, 72
  act for the protection of Islip and Huntington.................... 69
  who may plant in Great South bay.................................. 67
  taking away by party other than planter................... 68, 69
  when right to plant forfeited... 68
  inhabitant may use land for planting............................... 68
  oysters planted on natural growth of clams.............. 68, 69
  privilege to plant, etc., in Huntington, repealed............... 69
  inhabitants of Hempstead and Jamaica may plant............ 72
  to have exclusive property in beds................................. 72
  non-residents to use water.. 72
  quantity of land allowed inhabitant, how marked and defined.. 72, 73
  number of bushels to be planted to the acre.................... 72
  limitation of time for planting...................................... 73
  certificate, how filed.. 73
  annual rent to town.. 73
  how applied.. 73
  abandonment.. 74
  dredging, etc.. 74
  planting of, regulated in Jamaica and Hempstead............ 74
  who may plant.. 74
  when inhabitant entitled to bed.................................... 75
  planting by non-resident... 92
  gathering by non-resident... 92
  taken or disturbed... 92
  catching by dredge or dray.. 82
                (*See Shell-Fish.*)

OYSTER BEDS,
  survey and map of, to be made 51, 52
  application for, by occupants....................................... 52
  protector of, located in State.. 54
  deposit of certain acids, etc., injurious to oyster culture, prohibited, 54
  proviso... 54
  deposit of ashes, garbage, etc., in certain waters, prohibited...... 54
  penalties of violation of certain acts in regard to............... 54
  when to be granted in Gardner's and Peconic bays........... 56
  application for, not to cover more than three acres........... 56
  cost per acre.. 56
  deeds to be recorded.. 56
  in Great South bay.. 57
  any inhabitant of Islip or Babylon may locate lot.............. 57
  owners of oysters in beds in Great South bay.................. 57
  oyster commission to locate... 58
  decision as to location, etc.. 59
  expenses of locating and yearly rent.............................. 59
  certificate of location... 59

OYSTER BEDS — (Continued), PAGE.
   when rights to possession may be determined..... 59
   certificate of fact........ 59
   interest in lot assignable 60

OYSTER COMMISSION,
   authorized to appoint State oyster protector.......... 54, 55
   how appointed........ 57, 58
   to grant lots in Great South bay 58
   term of office 58
   official oath......... 58
   bond......... 58
   refusal to serve......... 58
   vacancy, how filled... 58
   to locate lot......... 58
   to cause survey and maps to be made......... 59
   decision as to location, etc., final......... 59
   expenses of location and yearly rent......... 59
   certificate of location......... 59
   when to determine right to possession 59
   certificate of the fact......... 59
   compensation of......... 59, 60
   to account......... 60
   term of present commission......... 60

PANTHER,
   State bounty for......... 25
   proof of killing......... 25
   bounty, how paid......... 26

PARADOX LAKE,
   catching black bass in......... 19

PARTRIDGE,
   season for......... 13, 28
   netting and snaring forbidden......... 14
   when may be sold or had in possession 28
   season for, in certain counties......... 34
   penalties......... 35
   violations......... 35
   protected in Chautauqua and Cattaraugus counties......... 36
   season for, suspended in Niagara county......... 36

PECONIC BAY,
   certain oyster beds in, protected......... 54
   interest of State to, conditionally released to county 55
   restrictions to concession of......... 55

PENALTIES,
   how recovered......... 26, 27
   where suit to be brought; costs of suit......... 26, 27, 30
   district attorney to prosecute judgments; how enforced..... 26, 27, 31
   if collected, how distributed......... 26, 27

INDEX.   121

PENALTIES — (Continued),   PAGE.
distribution 32, 38
for violation song and wild bird laws 34
how applied 34
in Chautauqua, how divided 32
how recovered for violation of game laws in Chautauqua and Cattaraugus counties 36
how disposed of 42
how recovered 42
for killing or injuring fish while passing over dams 82
for neglect of owners to alter dams at proper time 82
for railroad companies violating provisions, etc 89

PEWEE,
season for 32
had in possession or exposing for sale 32

PHEASANTS,
defined as game birds 33

PHŒBE BIRD,
season for 32
had in possession or exposing for sale 32
when not to be taken 38

PICKEREL,
in Lake George 20
spearing in certain lakes 21
possession of, when prohibited 43

PIERS,
(See Wharves.)

PIKE,
possession of, when prohibited 43

PIKE PERCH,
season for 19
in Lake Erie and Niagara river 19
exposing for sale in Erie county 19
may be sold at any time when brought from out of the State 39

PILOT COMMISSIONERS,
to remove fish-poles in New York harbor 47

PINNATED GROUSE,
(See Prairie Chicken.)

PLAYING,
on Sabbath 92

PLOVER,
defined as game birds 33
season for, in certain counties 35
protected in Chautauqua and Cattaraugus counties 36

16

INDEX.

POLICE JUSTICE,   PAGE.
    justice of the peace, magistrate..................................... 8
    to hear and try certain actions without delay...................... 8

POLLUTING STREAMS,
    prohibited.. 22, 33

PORT BAY,
    fishing in... 20, 21

POTS,
    having in possession on certain shores in Saugerties............ 41

POUND,
    when duty of commissioners to confiscate........................ 5
                       (See Nets and Weirs.)

POWER OF FIRE WARDEN,
    to destroy fences, etc. 88
    check fires, etc... 88

POWER OF SUPERVISOR,
    to destroy fences, etc... 88
    check fires 88

PRAIRIE CHICKEN,
    season for... 13
    netting or snaring forbidden................................... 14
    when may be sold or had in possession.......................... 28
    defined as game bird... 33

PRIVATE PARKS,
    sign boards to be erected...................................... 24
    penalty for injuring sign board............................ 24, 25
    game in 23, 24, 25
    trespassing prohibited.................................. 23, 24, 25
    hunting and fishing in, prohibited...................... 23, 24, 25
    poisoning fish in....................................... 23, 24, 25
    poisoning game in....................................... 23, 24, 25
    dogs in 25, 26
    board of supervisors not to legislate for...................... 28

PRIVATE STREAMS,
    fishing in, prohibited... 24
    notice of privacy of streams to be given................... 23, 24
    sign boards to be erected...................................... 24
    penalty for injuring sign boards........................... 24, 25

PRIVATE WATERS,
    defined.. 16

PROPAGATION,
    artificial, of shad, white-fish and salmon-trout, to be established, 3

INDEX.

PROTECTORS,
 appointment of 5
 powers, salary, etc... 5
 jurisdiction of 5
 to hold office during pleasure of commission 5
 one to be designated as chief protector 5
 to keep a daily record 5
 other protectors to be under supervision of chief.................. 5
 chief protector to give bond....................................... 5
 bond of other protectors... 5
 chief to issue orders to subordinates............................ 5, 6
 duties of, not to be interfered with by other business or employment 6
 duties of, to enforce laws of State................................ 6
 duties of, to enforce laws of county............................... 6
 supervisor 6
 chief to be assigned desk room 6
 shall have power to employ clerical service........................ 6
 salary of chief protector 6
 salaries of other protectors....................................... 6
 action to be begun by order of...................................... 6
 shall have power to prosecute...................................... 6
 may at certain times employ counsel.............................. 6, 7
 chief to approve the employment of counsel........................ 7
 one-half of fine to be paid to protector who brings suit........... 7
 power to arrest.. 7, 8
 chief may apply to attorney-general for construction of statutes... 8
 chief to report to commissioners of fisheries incompetency, etc., of
  subordinates.. 8
 to make monthly statements to chief 8
 to report annually to the commissioners of fisheries 8
 expenses not paid except upon certificate of chief 8
 duty to destroy nets, pounds, etc., when used in violation of law.. 9

PUBLIC SPORTS,
 on Sabbath 92

PUBLIC STREAMS,
 provision for the purpose of restocking............................ 49

PUNISHMENT,
 for attempting to catch fish within prescribed limits.............. 79
 for neglect to comply with order of forest commission............. 88
 for willful setting of fires 89

QUAIL,
 season for 13, 28
 kill, expose for sale, or had in possession........................ 13
 killing in the counties of Montgomery, Schenectady, Saratoga or
  Albany.. 13
 netting or snaring prohibited...................................... 14
 season for selling or having in possession 28

QUAIL — (Continued),   PAGE.
    defined as wild birds 33
    season for, suspended in Niagara county 36
    shooting of, on Robins Island, season for..... 37

QUEENS COUNTY,
    hunting wild deer in.......................... 10
    season for game............................... 34
    certain oyster beds in, protected 53
    use or occupation of land without lease in.... 61
    license for planting oysters in............... 61
    planting of oysters in 65
    condition on which inhabitants may plant and own beds.......... 65
    who may use land for planting 65, 66
    conditions................................ 65, 66
    proceedings in, in case of prosecution........ 66
    when abandonments, etc., cause forfeiture of . 66
    natural beds in Little Neck bay............... 67
    removal of oysters............................ 67
    planting of oysters in, regulated........ 72, 73, 74, 75

RABBIT,
    season for.................................... 13
    kill, expose for sale, or had in possession... 13
    killing or hunting with ferrets............... 13
    when may be sold or had in possession 28
    killing, wounding, or trapping in cemetery, etc 93

RAILS,
    defined as "game birds"....................... 33

RAIL BIRD,
    season for, in certain counties............... 35

RAILROAD COMPANIES,
    to cut and burn grass, etc 88
    penalty for violating requirements, etc....... 89
    ·duties in case of drought, etc............... 89
    prohibited from depositing fire, coals, etc., on tracks............ 89

RALLIDÆ,
    defined as "game birds"....................... 33

RARITAN BAY,
    angling for menhaden regulated................ 47

RECORDS,
    of description of fire district............... 87
    of names of fire wardens...................... 87

RENSSELAER COUNTY,
    song and small birds 32

REPEAL,
    certain acts in regard to Chautauqua lake, repealed.............. 43

INDEX.

REWARDS,
how divided 26, 27

RICHMOND COUNTY,
song and small birds 32
game protected.. 34
non-residents not to shoot game without license................... 34
angling for menhaden in Raritan bay.............................. 47
certain oyster beds in, protected 53
act to protect planting of oysters and clamming in and about, 69, 70, 71
action, etc., for violation of............................... 69, 70

ROBIN,
kill, expose for sale or had in possession 14, 32, 38
season for.. 32

ROBIN ISLAND,
season for quail 37

RUFFED GROUSE,
(See Partridge.)

RULES,
to be posted and replaced by forest agents, etc................. 89
for prevention of forest fires, etc............................. 89
printing and posting same 89
for protection, etc., to be established by forest commissioners..... 91

SABBATH-BREAKING,
punishment.. 92

SALMON,
in certain lakes.. 20
caught in net to be returned to water........................... 40
catching of, by angling... 40
season for.. 40
dams altered for benefit of 81
(See Trout.)

SALMON RIVER,
fishing in 21

SALT-WATER BASS,
exception 19
(See Bass.)

SAND PIPERS,
defined as "game birds"... 33
season for, in certain counties 35

SARATOGA COUNTY,
location of forest preserve..................................... 83

SAUGERTIES,
having nets, etc., in possession on shores of waters in 41

SCIENTIFIC PURPOSE,
certain bird not protected when killed for 38

SCHOOL-HOUSES, ETC.,   PAGE.
    proviso as to tax... 91

SCHOOL TRUSTEES,
    duties as to posting and replacing rules.......................... 81

SCHOHARIE RIVER,
    fish-way across.. 78, 79
    by whom constructed... 78, 79
    appropriation.. 79

SCIENTIFIC INVESTIGATION,
    nests and eggs for.. 33
    certificate to collect eggs, etc.................................... 33
    how granted.. 33
    conditions.. 33
    penalty for violation of... 33
    terms of.. 33
    term thereof... 33
    certain birds excepted from...................................... 33
    protection of certain birds....................................... 33
    on Long Island... 33

SEINES,
    using in Cattaraugus creek regulated............................ 46
                      (See Nets.)

SENECA RIVER,
    catching bass and muscalonge in................................ 19
    fish-way across.. 76, 77
    to be built by superintendent of public works.................... 76
    appropriation.. 77
    fish-way across.. 76, 77
    by whom constructed.. 77
    plans, how approved.. 78

SENECA LAKE,
    catching fish in... 20

SET LINE,
    having in possession on certain shores in Saugerties............. 41
                      (See Nets.)

SIGN-BOARDS,
    commissioners of fisheries, required to erect................. 21, 79

SKANEATELES LAKE,
    catching black bass in... 19

SHAD,
    not to be taken from Hudson river except at certain period....... 4
    season for, in part of Hudson river.............................. 41

SHAD POLES,
    act not to apply to.. 48

INDEX.

SHELLS, PAGE.
    in South bay... 71, 72

SHELL-FISH,
    granting of franchises for culture of................................ 52
    commissioner of fisheries to make rules and regulations in regard
        to cultivation of.. 52
    interest of State in certain waters conditionally released to Suffolk
        county for the cultivation of..................................... 55
    in Peconic and Gardner's bays................................. 55, 56
    disturbing bottom or injuring shell-fish a misdemeanor............ 57
    owners or lessees of land in Jamaica bay may plant................ 63
    locality for, to be designated.. 63
    in Hempstead and Jamaica..................................... 63, 64
    inhabitants of Hempstead and Jamaica may plant................. 63
    bed not to exceed two acres.. 63
    not lawful for other than planter to remove...................... 64
    arrest and bail for removal... 64
    rights and privileges forfeited 64
    act to regulate in Richmond county............................... 69
    taking by dredge or drag... 92
    taking by non-resident.. 92
    taking or disturbing... 92

SHELL-FISH COMMISSION,
    certain appointee of commissioner of fisheries to be.............. 51
    shall complete survey and map 51
    to ascertain the occupants of certain lands 52
    power to grant lands 52
    to occupant of same 52
    proviso... 52
    appointment of additional commissioner 52
    to be from Queens, Kings or Suffolk counties................... 52

SHERIFF,
    duties of.. 27, 28, 70
    penalties for failure to act.. 28
    powers of.. 27, 28
    in Richmond county, when to seize apparatus.............. 69, 70
    to hold apparatus seized, as under attachment.................. 70
    to notify the owner of such seizure 70
    with warrant and complaint 70, 71

SHINERS,
    catching with nets in Lake Keuka................................ 16
    may be caught with net in Lake Ontario 45

SHOOTING,
    on Sabbath 92

SHORE BIRDS,
    defined as "game birds" 33
    season for, in certain counties.................................... 35

INDEX.

SCHROON LAKE,
    catching black bass in 19

SNIPE,
    defined as "game birds" 33
    protected in Chautauqua and Cattaraugus counties................ 36

SNOW BIRDS,
    season for.. 32
    had in possession or exposing for sale 32

SONG BIRDS,
    collected for scientific purposes 14
    season for, kill, exposing for sale or had in possession of.... 14, 31, 32
    nests and eggs of 33
    scientific purposes... 33
    when not to be killed... 38

SOUTH BAY,
    preservation of shell-fish in 71, 72
    use of dredge or drag in, prohibited 71
    taking shell-fish from private beds regulated 71, 72
    penalties 72
    possession of dredge, evidence....................................... 72
    time for taking oysters, spawn, etc................................. 72

SPARROWS,
    not protected 33

SPAWN,
    taking from private hatcheries...................................... 17
    in Adirondack region.. 18

SPRUCE GROUSE,
                (See Canada Partridge.)

SQUIRREL,
    gray, season for 28
    black, season for... 28
    killing, wounding or trapping in cemeteries, etc................ 93

STAKES,
    used for making oyster beds 93
    removed or destroyed 93

STATE DAMS,
    fish-ways constructed in, by superintendent..................... 81

STATE LANDS,
    in forest preserve, assessed, etc 90
    assessment approved by comptroller............................ 90
    assessment of, corrected by comptroller 90
    taxes paid by State treasurer....................................... 91

STATE OYSTER PROTECTOR,
    how appointed 54, 55
    duties and salaries... 55

INDEX. 129

STATE OYSTER PROTECTOR — (Continued), PAGE.
   traveling expenses, etc., how paid 55
   assistant protectors... 55
   how paid 55

STATEN ISLAND,
   to regulate the taking of oysters and clams on south side of........ 65

STATE TREASURER,
   to pay tax upon State lands.. 91

STATE TREASURY,
   one half proceeds paid to county treasurer to be paid into State
      treasury.. 7

STATEN ISLAND,
   season for robins and larks 33

STARLING,
   kill, expose for sale or had in possession 14, 32
   season for... 32
   when not to be killed or had in possession.......................... 38

STREAMS OF WATER,
   to be examined by commissioner for the propagation of trout..... 3

STRIPED BASS (Fresh water),
   weight and length of 19

STRIPED BASS (Salt water),
   weight and length of 19

ST. LAWRENCE COUNTY,
   hunting wild deer in... 10
   location of forest preserve 83

ST. LAWRENCE RIVER,
   catching bass and muscalonge in..................................... 19

STOCKING,
   with trout in Adirondack fish hatcheries............................ 49

STEUBEN COUNTY,
   catching minnows for bait in Keuka lake............................. 16
   · having trout in possession or offering for sale.................... 43

SUBSCRIPTION,
   forest commission authorized to receive............................. 91

SUCKERS,
   catching with nets on Lake Keuka.................................... 16
   in canals.. 20
   season for... 21
   killing with spear in certain lakes 21
   may be caught with net in Lake Ontario.............................. 45
   fishing for, in Cayuga and Keuka lakes.............................. 46

17

SUFFOLK COUNTY,

	PAGE.
hunting wild deer in	10
season for game	34
certain oyster beds protected	53
interest of State in certain waters conditionally released to	55
concession not to interfere with rights of commissioners of land office	53
other restrictions	55
board of supervisors to appoint commissioner of shell fisheries in	55
deeds to be recorded in	56
use of dredge or drag in South bay prohibited	71
taking shell-fish from private beds	71, 72
penalties	72
possession of drag, evidence	72
time for taking spawn, etc	72

SULLIVAN COUNTY,

location of forest preserve	83

SUNDAY,

shooting, trapping, hunting or caging birds, or beasts prohibited	26
having in possession implements for same prohibited	26

SUPERINTENDENT,

to construct fish-ways in State dams	81

SUPERINTENDENT OF PUBLIC WORKS,

duties as to construction of fish-ways	80

SUPERVISORS,

no authority over land and waters wholly private	28
to authorize election of game constables in town	29
in Kings county	29
to audit and allow costs of suit	30
to raise tax	27
may employ special detectives	27
may pay awards	27
may make laws for the protection of game	27, 28
may prohibit hunting and fishing in county	27, 28
publication of laws and ordinances	28
to make provision for fish hatching in Otsego lake	37, 38
board of, to appoint commissioners of shell fisheries in Suffolk county	55
commissioners to be residents of certain towns	55
other restrictions	55, 56
to regulate costs for oyster beds	56
to require bond from oyster commissioner	58
in Gravesend and Flatlands, to grant permits	75, 76
duty to report spoliation, injuries, etc., to district attorney	86
protectors of lands, etc	86
to report proceedings to forest commission	86
as fire wardens	87

INDEX.

SUPERVISORS — (*Continued*),   PAGE.
  power to appoint fire wardens in towns, exposed to damage, etc... 87
  to report proceedings to forest commission........................ 88
  power to destroy fences, etc....................................... 88
  to report fires, etc... 88
  duties with regard to causes of fires, etc......................... 88
  duties as to posting and replacing rules.......................... 89
  to receive assessment of State lands, etc...................... 90, 91

SURF BIRDS,
  defined as "game birds"... 33

SURVEY,
  commissioners of fisheries to have survey of oyster beds completed, 51
  requisite for, in Suffolk county.................................. 56

SWALLOW,
  season for.. 32
  had in possession or exposing for sale............................ 32

SWANS,
  defined as "game birds"... 33

TATLERS,
  defined as "game birds"... 33

TAX,
  may be raised... 27
  supervisors to raise tax.. 27
  proviso as to, school-houses, etc................................. 91
  approved by... 91
  upon State lands paid by State treasurer.......................... 91
  credit by county treasurers....................................... 91

TEAL,
  season for, in Chautauqua county.................................. 35

THRUSH,
  season for.. 32
  had in possession or exposing for sale............................ 32
  when not to be taken.. 38

TONAWANDA CREEK,
  taking fish from.. 20

TOWN ASSESSOR,
  in regard to filing copy of assessment rolls, etc................. 90
  additional statement.. 90

TRESPASSING,
  prohibited... 15, 24, 25
  notice to be given not to trespass....................... 15, 24, 25
  sign boards to be erected.................................... 15, 24
  penalty for injuring sign boards.................................. 25
  what it includes.. 85

INDEX.

TROUT, PAGE.
    streams to be examined for the propagation of 3
    in Lake Ontario, Niagara river.................................. 15
    in private waters.. 15
    how to be caught... 15, 16
    speckled..................................... 15, 16, 17, 18, 20
    brook.. 15, 16, 17, 18, 20
    salmon 15, 16
    setting net near mouth of Oswego river......................... 16
    catching with net in Lake Keuka............................... 16
    speckled, brook or salmon through the ice...................... 16
    in Lake Ontario and Niagara excepted.......................... 16
    speckled, brook, California and brown, season for.............. 16
    size of.. 17
    in Lake Ontario during spawning season 17
    not to be molested in spawning season......................... 17
    catching in Lake Ontario for stocking 17
    catching for stocking private ponds............................ 17
    killing, exposing for sale or had in possession................. 17
    brook, brown, speckled, California and salmon, in Adirondack
        region.. 18
    from forest preserve, in possession............................ 18
    salmon or lake, season for, in Lake George..................... 18
    salmon or lake, season for 18
    in certain lakes 20
    shutting or drawing off waters................................ 20
    exposing for sale or having in possession, in Steuben county.... 43
    when caught in Lake Ontario by net........................... 45
    provisions for the purpose of restocking public streams with ... 49
    stocking waters in Adirondacks with 49
    restocking in Adirondacks with 51
    fish hatcheries 51

TROUT (Salmon),
    may be sold at any time when brought from out of State........ 39

ULSTER COUNTY,
    location of forest preserve..................................... 83

VENISON.
    may be sold, transported or had in possession 28

WALKILL RIVER,
    fishing in... 21

WALL-EYED PIKE,
                   (See Pike Perch.)

WARRANTS,
    courts to issue, violation of game law 30, 38
    how issued 30
    when issued.. 30

INDEX.

WARRANTS — (Continued),   PAGE.
  for non-residents... .... 30, 39,
  search warrants 36, 39, 47
  game constable to arrest with or without, in Washington and Essex
    counties.. 44

WARREN COUNTY,
  location of forest preserve 83

WASHINGTON COUNTY,
  power of game constable.. 44
  location of forest preserve.. 83

WATER,
  pollution of, prohibited 32, 33
  rights to surplus, etc... 80

WEIR,
  when duty of commissioner to confiscate........................... 5
  using in Raritan bay regulated.................................... 47
  use of, in New York harbor, regulated............................. 48
  setting or attaching 92

WESTCHESTER COUNTY,
  certain oyster beds in, protected 54

WILD BIRDS,
  killing or catching.. 32
  nests and eggs of.. 33
  scientific purposes 33

WILD DEER,
  protector may arrest for violation of laws for protection of...... 7, 8
  sale of.. 10
  possession of 10
  transportation of 10
  traps and spring guns... 10
  protection of fawn.. 10
  hunting in St. Lawrence and Delaware counties.................... 10
  crusting and yarding prohibited................................... 10
  in Queens and Suffolk counties.................................... 10
  hunting with dogs... 10
  hunting season.. 10
  head or feet of, when severed from the carcass 11
                           (See Deer.)

WILD DUCK,
  killing.. 11
  exposing for sale... 11
  having in possession.. 11
  in the waters of Long Island...................................... 11
  killing with swivel or punt gun 12

INDEX.

WILD DUCK — (*Continued*),   PAGE.
  using other device than gun.. 12
  in Great South bay.. 12
  in Peconic bay.. 12
  in Shinnecock bay... 12
  in Lake Ontario... 12
  in St. Lawrence and Hudson rivers................................. 12

WILD FOWLS,
  using boats, etc.. 12
  in Long Island sound, Gardner's and Peconic bays, Lake Ontario
    and the Hudson river... 12
  hunting with decoys, floating batteries, bow-house, etc............ 12

WILD GAME,
  land set apart for.. 91

WILD GOOSE,
  in Long Island sound, Gardner's and Peconic bays, Lake Ontario
    and the Hudson river... 12
  shooting out of floating battery, machine or device............... 12
  season for, in Chautauqua county.................................. 35

WILD TURKEY,
  defined as "game birds"... 33

WHARVES,
  act not to apply to the filling in of land under water granted by
    the State... 48
  nor to sweeping or washing boats, etc 48

WOLVES,
  State bounty for.. 25
  proof of killing.. 25
  bounty, how paid.. 26

WOODCOCK,
  season for.. 13
  in Oneida and Delaware counties................................... 13
  when may be sold or had in possession............................. 28
  defined as "game bird".. 33
  protected in Chautauqua and Cattaraugus counties.................. 36

WOODPECKER,
  kill, expose for sale or had in possession.................. 14, 32
  season for.. 32
  when not to be taken.. 38

WREN,
  kill, expose for sale or had in possession.................. 14, 32
  season for.. 32
  when not to be taken.. 38

INDEX.

YATES COUNTY,
PAGE.
catching minnows for bait in Keuka lake.......................... 16

YELLOW BIRD,
kill, expose for sale or had in possession....................... 14, 32
season for.. 32
when not to be taken 38

YELLOW HAMMER,
season for.. 31
had in possession or exposed for sale........................... 32
when not to be taken 38

YELLOW LAKE,
spearing in 21

www.ingramcontent.com/pod-product-compliance
Lightning Source LLC
Chambersburg PA
CBHW030357170426
43202CB00010B/1403